On the Road To . . .

An Amazing True Story

Life is not a Destination.
It is a Journey.

Roger R. Rinker

xulon
PRESS

Dedication

This book is dedicated to my lovely, caring, considerate, and precious wife Nancy. She has journeyed the many miles "On the Road To. . ." alongside of me. She has always been there to lend a hand and speak a word of encouragement, never once turning her back on me, even during the darkest hours.

"Lord, I thank You for this wonderful woman You have given me as my wife and the mother of our two sons, Rodney and Duane."

To my two daughter-in-laws and all my grandchildren and great grandchild, I say, "Thank you, and I love you."

This book is also a tribute to my father, Roland T. Rinker, who went to be with the Lord in 1988. Thanks, Dad, for a lesson you taught me many years ago when I was a young child.

Special thanks go to my mother, Althea, who is still going strong in her golden years. Thanks, Mom, for all the sacrifices you made, so that as a child, I could have the things you did not have.

And to all those who shared my life's journey as I traveled and continue to travel "On the Road To ...", may God continue to richly bless each of you.

Introduction:

On the Road To . . .

Life is Not a Destination.
It is a Journey.

As a young boy at the age of four, I recall my father coming home from work in our 1939 Plymouth sedan. Dad's place of employment was only two miles from our home. After a long, hot day Dad would jump into our car and make this trip on a newly resurfaced macadam roadway. For the early 1940s this was one of the better roads in the area in which we lived. This road served him well. It met his need, providing a way for him to go work and back home again.

Having just moved into this dwelling place was a real challenge for the three of us. This structure, as I will call it, had been neglected for quite some time and was in need of major repairs. Portions had to be torn down due to deterioration. There was no running water. Water had to be hand pumped from a cistern which had not been cleaned in years. We had no inside bathroom facilities, only a one-seater outside, and the heating system was a coal stove which was also used for cooking and baking.

Had Mom and Dad purchased this structure for a place to house chickens, it would have been ready for them at the time of settlement as some had already found a nesting place there along with the mice and rats.

No, that is not what Mom and Dad had in mind. It was not to be a chicken coop. This was to be our home, our dwelling place in spite of what the exterior and interior looked like. They were determined, they had a vision, and they had a plan. Nothing was going to stop them from turning this structure into a home. It was all we had, but it was not the end of the road for us.

After months of hard work, and many blisters and numerous pains, this structure became our home. Outside of the actual structure, weeds and trees had taken over everywhere and were covered with poison ivy. Little did I know that my body would have a negative reaction to poison ivy, in a matter of a few days, my body was covered with this poison, which left me in a state of misery.

Time moved on as it does and with time came changes. My life was about to head down a new road, a new journey. I recall one early spring day my dad saying, "Son, come July we're going on a vacation." "Vacation," I thought, "what's that? Does this mean we will have to pack everything we have worked so hard for and move to another place?"

"No," I was informed. "It is going to be a time for the family to get into our car, head out and get on the road and drive to a place where we can relax and do some fishing." This would be a place I had never been before. Excitement grew in me as the weeks passed by, and finally the day arrived.

Dad came home from work at 5:15 in the afternoon as usual. We quickly loaded everything into the car, including all that Mom had prepared, and we headed out "on the road to Promise Land". This place, as it is named, is an area in the mountains of northeastern Pennsylvania. Excitement raced throughout my body as we started our journey of about sixty miles.

It was not long before the road ahead of us was no longer a thrill. Soon everything came to a halt as the car had developed some mechanical problems. Smoke started pouring out from under the hood. My first thought was, "Now what? Is this what vacations are all about? I thought Dad said it was going to be a time to relax and go fishing."

"No problem," Dad assured me. "All we need is some water for the radiator." After a few moments, having added more water to the radiator, we were on our way once again. It wasn't long before we had to pull over for the second time. More smoke, more water, and off we go again.

Then I popped the big question, "Dad, are we there yet?" By this time I was questioning Dad if the road to Promise Land was the one we passed a few hours ago. Dad answered, "No son, we did not miss the road," and he assured me that we would make it. Make it we did, but not in the amount of time Dad had said it would take.

Looking back some sixty years in time, I now realize the lesson I learned that day. As long as we don't give up, regardless of circumstances, if we persevere, we will reach "Promise Land".

Today as I travel, I'm overwhelmed by all the vehicles on the roads. There are highways, with eight and ten lanes all in one direction. People are traveling, north, south, east, and west, and in many places the traffic moves at a snail's pace, even with all the major highways. Where is everyone going, and why are they in such a hurry? God forbid that you should slow down to try to read a road sign. Could it be they are all headed or looking for "the road to Promise Land"?

Road signs today are of great importance to me. Getting lost, or as I like to phrase it, "Just thought I'd try a new way," is not fun. When my wife says, "Roger, this is the second time we passed that house, and the same people are sitting on the front porch," I know I'm lost, and she is right. What about the signs along the way? Was I too preoccupied on my way, "on the road to . . . " to take heed to the signs?

Whenever or wherever we travel today, there are many signs we encounter. There are signs letting us know the speed limit, dangerous situations ahead, where to enter or exit, and places we are forbidden to go. All these signs are there to assist us in decisions we will face as we travel "On the Road To . . .".

Contents

Chapter 1

On the Road to Growing Up

"Train up a child in the way he should go, and when he is old he will not depart from it."
(Proverbs 22:6)

These words were written about King Solomon as recorded in **I Kings 3:12b**:

"...There has not been anyone like you before you, nor shall any like you arise after you."

In I Kings 4:29-34, King Solomon is referred to as being **"wiser than all men."**

Training up a child means the parent graciously invests time in that child by implanting whatever wisdom, love, and discipline is needed for the child to become fully committed to God.

Parents have a responsibility to train their children according to their children's personality, gifts, and aspirations. Children need to be taught to avoid whatever natural tendencies they might have, that would prevent them from totally committing themselves to the Lord. The early years of a child's development are very important. What is sown into a child's life will reproduce itself in later years.

King Solomon's words are not to be taken lightly. Remember God said he, King Solomon, is called "wiser than all men." These words should be taken as guidelines as we train up our children.

I pause here as my mind goes back in time. What did I miss because I was not taught by a Christian father? Oh yes, my dad did know of God, he loved his wife and children, and he was a good provider. My father did teach me principles of life that I will never forget.

How did Dad know so much? What truths could his father have taught him, since he was a man who hated God and godly principles? His father, as I was told, worked nights at the Bethlehem Steel Mill and farmed by day. It was said that he would stand and curse God, because it rained on his freshly-cut hay field, or at times he would curse God, because it didn't rain on his crops, causing a poor harvest. Sin had entered his life, and he was deceived by Satan. My grandfather, however, did provide a place of shelter for my parents and me.

It was on this farm that I first learned how to ride a bicycle and also at the age of three was taught how to drive a farm tractor. Life was different as we lived primarily on the things we raised on the farm. All our vegetables were home-grown. We had hogs and beef cattle for our supply of meat, and we also had chickens, which produced eggs and meat for us. Our cows provided us with our daily milk and with the cream, which we churned into butter. Fresh baked bread, cakes, and pies were also featured items at meal times.

It was a sad day for my parents when they found out my grandfather had been in an accident and with him was a female with whom he was having an affair. This eventually led to my parents moving out of the home, taking with them my grandmother who lived with us for many years.

This hurtful situation between my dad and his father created a huge wall between them. In fact, from that day forward, they never spoke one word to each other again. Respect for one another had been shattered, which only added to my grandfather's choice of lifestyle.

Dad was not going to let this root take hold in his life. Dad was different. He had not been taught to honor and respect others, yet he not only demanded it from his children, he lived it.

These were the seeds sown into my life as a child: work hard; always give and do your best; do unto others as you would expect them to do to you; don't ever be late for a meal or a meeting; nothing in life is free; do as you said you would do; your word must be like a legal document; "don't lie 'cuz' I'll find out the truth"; "when we do go to church, you will wear your best"; and "yes, you will sit with your mother and me, and you will be quiet."

Of all the things my Dad taught me, there is one thing that always stayed fresh in my mind. When Dad said, "You better," I had better do it, because Dad only spoke once. I knew I had better act accordingly or action was about to be taken. There was no back talk or questioning. Dad expected action, not excuses, on my part.

My King Solomon in my early years was my Dad. Although he was not a Christian at this point in time of my life, he was the best father to ever have lived. In fact, I see many so-called "Christian fathers" of today who could gain wisdom from his "training up a child."

Questions Only You Can Answer

Chapter 1 "On the Road to Growing Up"

How good of a memory do you have?

What do you remember as a child at the age of five?

Have any words of wisdom you were taught at that age had a positive effect on your life?

Do you remember the first vacation in which all of your family were involved?

Have you ever been guilty of asking the question, "Are we there yet?"

What difference do you see in the roads of today than when you were five?

Do you agree, "Life is not a destination, but a journey"?

Chapter 2

On the Road to Becoming a Youth

Solomon requests wisdom from God in **I Kings 3:9-12**:

> **"'Therefore give to Your servant an understanding heart to judge Your people, that I may discern between good and evil. For who is able to judge this great people of Yours?' The speech pleased the Lord, that Solomon had asked this thing.**
>
> **"Then God said to him: 'Because you have asked this thing, and have not asked long life for yourself, nor have asked riches for yourself, nor have asked the life of your enemies, but have asked for yourself understanding to discern justice, behold I have done according to your words; see, I have given you a wise and understanding heart, so that there has not been anyone like you before you, nor shall any like you arise after you.'"**

A few chapters later we read where King Solomon had made a mess out of his life. He allowed an "I" attitude to dominate his life. "I am the greatest, and there will never be anyone as wise as I am." His prideful attitude got him away from God, and he started making confessions of his weaknesses.

> **"Whatever my eyes desired I did not keep from them. I did not withhold my heart from any pleasure, for my heart rejoiced in all my labor; and this was my reward from all my labor."**
> **(Ecclesiastes 2:10)**

King Solomon rejected wisdom, the wisdom he had received firsthand from God Himself. It was a perfect time for King Solomon to a have pity-party. "Lord, look at the mess I have made and the fruits of my labor."

> **"Then I looked on all the works that my hands had done and on the labor in which I had toiled; and indeed all was vanity and grasping for the wind. There was no profit under the sun."**
> **(Ecclesiastes 2:11)**

What had gone wrong? Had God failed him? He had everything the world could offer: wealth, menservants, maidservants, singers, and the special treasures of kings and provinces, but still something was missing.

In chapter one, I related to principles my father taught me as a young child. As I grew in years, reaching the preteen years, I started putting into practice what I had been taught: work hard and always give and do your best. At the age of ten I started working summers for a local farmer. This man was a trustee/elder/deacon of a local church and was highly respected by the community. He was willing to give me a chance to prove myself as a hard worker through all types of working conditions. From early morning until late afternoon I would toil in the hot sun handling bales of hay and straw until my hands ached with pain, blisters one on top of another. It was hard work, but it was rewarding as I was being paid fifty cents an hour.

I was looking and planning ahead for my sixteenth birthday as that would entitle me to driving privileges. Dad had already informed me that if I wanted to drive at sixteen, it would be my responsibility to provide for my own vehicle. I was determined that by working hard I could save enough money to buy myself a car, which I did. The day finally came, and I celebrated my big sixteenth birthday. This day was a day of celebration as I took my driving test. I passed it, and that same day was "on the road to . . . ".

With all the excitement of now being sixteen, little did I remember about what I had been taught as a child. I now was a youth with a license to drive. Just like King Solomon, whatever my eyes desired, I did not keep from them. I did not withhold my heart from any pleasure. My heart rejoiced in all the labors, and this was my reward.

Hard work was producing. It brought me much pleasure as I had money to buy the finer things in life. Cars and young women soon consumed my life. I was a hit with all my friends. It was just a matter of time until I realized that I was facing a situation, being backed into a corner, that I didn't want or care for. Something had gone wrong. My life style was one that led me into an engagement with a young woman. I was only eighteen, and I knew neither of us knew what we were doing. I needed a way out, a way of escape. My mind said, "Get away. Things will change."

"Don't lie 'cuz' I'll find out the truth" kept going through my mind. These were the words I kept hearing repeatedly as these were words my father had implanted into my life as a child. My life was miserable. Lies started proceeding from my lips more frequently. I tried making excuses for things I was doing, and they were poor ones. In fact, my father and mother knew I was not telling the truth. My life was miserable!

"Train up a child in the way he should go, and when he is old he will not depart from it."
(Proverbs 22:6)

When is old? At what age are we exempt from the scriptures? For me at that time of my life, I thought it was at the age eighteen.

"Rejoice O young man, in your youth, and let your heart cheer you in the days of your youth; walk in the ways of your heart, and in the sight of your eyes; but know that for all these God will bring you into judgment." (Ecclesiastes 11:9)

King Solomon, for all the wisdom he had, knew he was headed for destruction. I realized that King Solomon was a human being, and I was no different. Peer pressure, hearing and responding to other voices, rather than the voice of God, had opened the doors for me to fall into temptations.

"Then I looked on all the works that my hands had done and on the labor in which I had toiled; and indeed all was vanity and grasping for the wind. There was no profit under the sun."
(Ecclesiastes 2:11)

When King Solomon reflected on his works, he began to realize that they were worthless. Reflecting back on my own life, I could see and understand the lesson I was being taught. A lesson at the age of eighteen I thought I had learned all too well was: **Pleasure satisfies only for a moment and accomplishes nothing.**

Questions Only You Can Answer

Chapter 2 "On the Road to Becoming a Youth"

What were your life's ambitions as a youth?

At the age of ten, how did you spend your summers and time off from school?

What patterns were being established in your life at that age?

Do you recall the first wages you were paid for working outside your home, and do you recall the hourly rate?

How important was your sixteenth birthday to you?

As a youth, are there parts of your past you would rather no one knew about?

As a youth, did peer pressures have an effect on you?

If given the chance, and one could go back in time, what would you do differently this time?

Chapter 3

On the Road to Running Away

I'm reminded of the words of the Psalmist David as he wrote:

> **"Do not remember the sins of my youth, nor my transgressions; according to Your mercy remember me, for Your goodness' sake, O Lord." (Psalm 25:7)**

How was the Lord going to forgive me for the mess I had made of my life? My parents were there for me, but I could not go to them. They just would not understand. I knew what I had been taught by my parents, school teachers, and Sunday School Teachers. They all had wisdom, however, I was eighteen and at the age of knowing it all.

Once again I'm reminded of some of the words of wisdom I had once been taught:

> **"My son, pay attention to my wisdom; lend your ear to my understanding, that you may preserve discretion, and your lips may keep knowledge. For the lips of an immoral woman drip honey,**

**and her mouth is smoother then oil; but in the end
she is bitter as wormwood, sharp as a two-edged
sword." (Proverbs 5:1-4)**

The trap had been set, and I was caught. I do not blame
everything that happened on this young woman, for I was at
fault as much as she was. I too was a human being and had
a problem with controlling my hormones. Run away! Run
away! That is what kept going through my mind. That was
the answer. Get as far away as you can, and the problem will
go away.

There was a poster I had once seen, and it started to reap-
pear in my mind. It was the one where Uncle Sam is pointing
at you and says, "I Want You". Here it was, my ticket to
freedom, a way to get away from a mess I had gotten myself
into. No one needed to know the truth of why I had enlisted.
I had an obligation to serve my country.

So off to the military I went. The United States Army
surely had the answers for my situation, I thought. For the
next six months I received my basic training at Fort Benning,
Georgia and then advanced training at Fort Lenordwood,
Missouri. No longer a "free to do as I please person", I was
being taught once again to submit to authority. I was now
"on the road to restoring my life."

After completion of my stateside training, I was shipped
off to Germany, where I spent the next thirty months. During
that time my connection and communication with this young
woman was growing distant. It was not long before I realized
it was not only time, but proper to break off our relationship.
Time had come and all I had to do was write the famous
letter. Write it I did, and it brought an end to an engagement
which should have never have happened in the first place.

Military life was great. After serving only eighteen
months in active duty, I was promoted to Specialist 5th class.
Hard work was paying off once again. Not only had I received

pay increases, but I had taken and passed additional proficiency tests adding additional income. Money was providing me with a great life. With the great life came consequences. Drinking became an everyday habit, and German beer, wine, gambling, and women were taking their toll. Being semiconscious to what was happening in my life, I thought, "Soon I'll be back where I was when I ran away from home, backed into a corner with no place to turn or hide."

What happened next to me was a blessing from God. My best friend Arthur and I decided we would fly home for Christmas in 1960. Arthur and I were the best of buddies. We had gone to school together, traveled with the same group of friends, and even dated the same girls. Sometime before leaving on our Christmas vacation, Arthur started writing to a young lady named Nancy from our hometown. I knew of her as my parents and hers used to travel and camp together. Upon arrival in Pennsylvania for our Christmas vacation, Nancy was contacted and asked if she could get a blind date for me. She replied she would.

The night came, and we were on our first double date. Arthur, my best friend, was with Nancy, and I was with the date Nancy had set up for me. This night was like no other night I had ever experienced. During the course of the night she, Nancy, pulled me to the side and said, "I've got a problem."

"What is it?" I asked. Her response sent my head spinning. This young lady was bold, not holding anything back as she said, "I want to be with you, not Arthur."

Here I was. I had just removed myself from a situation I should have never gotten myself into, and now this young woman says she wants to come into my life. Would this woman, someday possibly become an important part of my life?

Our relationship was moving at a fast pace. We were spending every available minute of everyday with each other. Not only were both our heads spinning, it was the fact that in only a few days I would be returning to Germany. I had to finish out my time of enlistment.

Was this love at first sight, love that would carry us through the next seven months until my tour of duty was completed? No more running away. I did a 180 degree turn and was now on the road to . . .

Saying good-bye was a moment of heartache, but we knew in our hearts, it was not a good-bye forever.

A side note: Arthur and I did remain the best of friends after that night. The day after the night of our double date, he made amends with a young lady he had been dating prior to our entering the military, and things were going great for him.

Questions Only You Can Answer

Chapter 3 "On the Road to Running Away"

Have you ever found yourself in the same place as the Psalmist David did in Psalm 25:

Have you asked God not to remember the sins of your youth?

Have you doubted the wisdom that was instilled into you?

Do you believe we will encounter traps through our earthly existence?

Do you believe running away can be the answer?

Did you or do you see yourself today as a "free to do as I please person?"

Do you have a hard time submitting to authority?

Has there been a Nancy in your life, one who spoke with so much boldness?

Chapter 4

On the Road to Choosing a Mate

"And you He made alive, who were dead in trespasses and sins, in which you once walked according to the course of this world, according to the prince of the power of the air, the spirit who now works in the sons of disobedience, among whom also we all once conducted ourselves in the lusts of our flesh, fulfilling the desires of the flesh and of the mind, and were by nature children of wrath, just as the others." (Ephesians 2:1-3)

I needed the mercy of God. Would God forgive me for all my stupid wrong doings? Could I be the one God had chosen as a husband for this young woman?

"Trust in the Lord, and do good; dwell in the land, and feed of His faithfulness. Delight yourself also in the Lord, and He shall give you the desires of your heart. Commit your way to the Lord, trust also in Him, and He shall bring it to pass." (Psalm 37:3-5)

My relationship with Nancy grew over those next seven months. We wrote letters to each other everyday. Oh how right it seemed. Yet I had reservations. Could this just be the flesh responding and were my hormones running wild again? Could I lay down my past and fulfill the role as a husband?

As soon as the ship docked and my feet touched the ground as I arrived back in the United States, I was off and running. This time not running away, but running toward someone.

With open arms Nancy greeted and accepted me. Joy started to flood my body. Truly I was in love, and yes, this was the woman God had sent to me. God did give me the desires of my heart. I trusted in Him, and He held nothing against me because of my past, and we started out "on the road to . . .".

Something I forgot to mention is that it says in **Psalm 37:5 "Commit your way to the Lord."** I trusted in God just as I had been taught by my Sunday School teacher many years before. Trust was not a problem, but committing my way to the Lord was where I had a challenge. My way seemed to be the only way I knew. Dad's advice to me kept ringing in my ears: "Work hard, always give and do your best, and nothing in life is free."

Was I ready to commit to something I knew very little about, meaning marriage? I knew that this marriage was about to give me the desires of my heart as God had promised.

Wedding plans were carried out in detail as we had planned. Our plan was really starting to take shape. Four months after being discharged from the U.S. Army on November 10, 1962 Nancy Carol Trump became Mrs. Roger Rinker.

Our wedding day was filled with joy and excitement as we stood in the presence of God and made a covenant to one another. We were committed that we would grow stronger in love, that we would care for each other, and nothing except death would ever separate us, a commitment that we have kept for over forty-seven years.

"He who finds a wife finds a good thing, and obtains favor from the Lord."(Proverbs 18:22)

Questions Only You Can Answer

Chapter 4 "On the Road to Choosing a Mate"

"Delight yourself also in the Lord, and He shall give you the desires of your heart." (Psalm 37:4)

If you are making plans concerning marriage, are they scripturally based, or are they based on the lusts of the flesh?

Have you been able to commit your ways to the Lord in all the decisions you have made in life?

Do you believe that he who finds a wife or husband, finds a good thing and obtains favor from the Lord?"

Do you believe in love at first sight?

Do you believe marriage should be a 50-50 relationship or 100-100, each giving his or her all, holding nothing back?

Do you really believe God will give you the desires of your heart?

Chapter 5

On the Road to Being a Provider

"But if anyone does not provide for his own, and especially for those of his household, he has denied the faith, and is worse off than an unbeliever." (I Timothy 5:8)

My father was a good provider for our family. He worked days at a local feed mill, a place where they made feed for animals. It was hard work and very dusty as the grains were ground into flour and animal feed. He also delivered these products to farmers and home owners and many times had to carry hundred pound sacks up into barns, down narrow paths in all kinds of weather.

After he came home from work and ate a meal with the family, Dad would either go outside and work in our large, almost one acre garden or do the necessary chores around the home. "Hard work will never hurt anyone," he kept confessing with an attitude that "I have a family, and I must provide for them."

Now my responsibility was to wear those same shoes. Our marriage brought with it many responsibilities, and I had an obligation to provide. Job hunting was not an exciting time for me. I did whatever I needed to do to find a job. Delivering bread, cakes, and doughnuts door-to-door for a local baking company was my first job after being married. My daily routine was getting up at three in the morning, driving to work, and then driving a truck loaded with these commodities. I would go door to door, home to home all day long delivering baked goods. It was a source of income for us. I was guaranteed a weekly salary for three weeks out of a month. I would get a percentage of the monies collected, and then the fourth week was settlement week. This meant that if my sales weren't up during the first three weeks, I wouldn't get much money at all the fourth week of the month. I did not keep this job long, because during the week of Christmas, which was the fourth week or settlement week, and because people were buying on credit, my cash receipts for that week were very low. They were so low in fact, that my take home check for that week was only eighteen dollars. I knew this was not going to make it for me.

It was not long before I was out job-hunting once again. This time I found employment in an electrical repair shop, rewinding electrical motors. My mother is one who is always doing something with her hands. A crotchet needle and some sort of yarn almost always can be found in her hand, as she has to keep her hands moving at all times. This is also part of my make-up which I inherited from her. However, using my hands to rewind motors was not what my hands were made for. This was not for me, as I headed out once again in search of another place of employment.

Next, I tried working at a fabrication plant, running a punch press, doing shift work. I could not stay there as I believed nights were made for sleeping.

A new job opportunity came as I was introduced to a foreman of a large highway construction company. The starting hourly wage was $2.50 per hour and working seventy to eighty hours per week was providing me with a good income for the early 1960s. Dad's words constantly rang in my ears: "Work hard; always give and do your best; do unto others as you would expect them to do to you." My work habits were about to pay off.

More blessings were on the way as I was promoted from general laborer to crane operator, bringing a pay increase to $9.50 from $2.50 per hour, which in the mid 60s was something to get excited about. Finally I was able to provide for my wife and two sons. A new home, numerous cars, a new pickup truck, recreational toys: motorcycles, snowmobiles, camping units, all found their way to our home. I was prospering in my eyes and in the eyes of the world.

As all this was happening, something of my past started taking root again. I not only had money to purchase these things, but I had pocket change with which I could buy an occasional drink. Drinking one drink now and then seemed harmless. Before I knew what had happened, I was once again hooked on alcohol. I needed something to keep me going as I was sometimes working up to 108 hours a week. I didn't have a problem with drinking. I was in control, at least that is what I kept telling myself.

"There is a way that seems right to a man, but its end is the way of death. The person who labors, labors for himself, for his hungry mouth drives him on." (Proverbs 16:25-26)

Once again I was being driven by the lusts of my flesh. To me prosperity was having all these things. I was working hard, and they were mine to enjoy. "Danger ahead" were signs I did not see or comprehend. Pushing myself to the limit was all I knew. I was providing for my family.

And then it happened. One night as I was returning home after a long day at work, I lost control of my new pick-up. Veering off the road, the truck came to rest with the front bumper being wrapped around and supporting, a telegraph pole, which I had just sheared off. This is where I found myself. The engine was torn from the frame, which along with the transmission, ended up inside the cab with me. With blood streaming down my face, arms and legs, and pain rushing through my body, I somehow was able to free myself from the wreckage. Crawling on hands and knees I made my way back to the road and ended up passing out, lying there on this dark country road. With no knowledge of an accident having just happened, as the truck was totally off the road, praise God, an alert driver spotted me lying in the street. He stopped, picked me up, and quickly drove me to the local hospital where I was admitted into the emergency room. As I lay there on the operating table, half conscious, I remember opening my eyes and looking around wondering where I was. All I could see was this great light shining before my eyes.

Had I had an experience like Saul on the road to Damascus? Was this the light that was before my eyes? Was this what it felt like to get knocked to the ground by God?

I began to look around and coming into focus were two shapes of what looked like men. Who were these men, and why were they standing in this light?

One of the men began to talk to me with a voice of authority and asked me, "Was your wife's maiden name Nancy Trump?"

I answered that it was, but I wondered why he was asking me such a question. Next he followed with a statement that shocked me to the bones. He informed me that he had been summoned to the scene of the accident and had found my wrecked pick-up truck. He also made the following statement to me, "Not only did we find your truck, but we also found everything you had left in the cab, all the empty beer cans and bottles of whiskey, which we have removed to save your reputation."

Slowly as I looked into this man's eyes something was telling me I had seen him before, and then I remembered. These same two uniformed policemen were the ones who awoke me from a nap I was taking two nights earlier. That night I was on my way home and had gotten very tired and decided to pull over and sleep for a few minutes. When these same two officers found me, I had pulled over and in doing so ended up jumping the curb and stopping my truck against a local place of business. They had informed me I had done nothing wrong, but that I needed to back my truck off the sidewalk, which I did.

My drinking problem had left me backed into another corner. My sinful life was exposed, and now I felt all alone, or was I really all alone? As I lay there on that operating table, for the first time in my life I admitted to God that I had a drinking problem. I said, "God if You are for real, then You take this problem from me, and I will serve You the rest of my life."

Up to this point in my life I was in control of my drinking habit, or at least that is what I had led myself to believe. A six pack and a fifth of whiskey were no problem for me to down in an hour as I drove home from work, yet I did not consider myself out-of-control or as having an addiction. With this encounter came the realization that I could no longer provide for my family on my own strength. I decided right there, that very night, hurting and bleeding and shaking, that something had to change. After being treated for minor cuts and bruises, and a few badly bruised ribs, I was released from the emergency room. Time heals all wounds, and mine healed quite rapidly.

Surely someone was watching out for me that night. Who had found me lying in the road and picked me up and transported me to the local hospital? No police report or hospital report contained the name of such a person, and by the way, the reason the police officer had asked me if my wife's maiden name was Nancy Trump was because he had graduated from high school with her. He had a heart of compassion and was more concerned in my getting help for my drinking problem than trying to create more problems in my life.

"In the day when I cried out, You answered me, and made me bold with strength in my soul." (Psalm 138:3)

Cry out I did! God, I was sure, heard me, but how was He going to respond?

Questions Only You Can Answer

Chapter 5 "On the Road to Being a Provider"

Who is depending on you as a provider?

Looking back in time, have you ever experienced a time of genuine need?

Ezekiel 28:4 "With your wisdom and your understanding you have gained riches for yourself, and gathered gold and silver into your treasuries." As a provider how much have you gained by your own wisdom and understanding?

Have you ever lost your foothold of a secure source of income?

How has God responded to your cries as you placed your financial burdens at His feet?

Can you relate to a time when God's hand of protection was upon you in the midst of a tragedy?

Chapter 6

On the Road to a New Beginning

"That if you confess with your mouth the Lord Jesus and believe in your heart that God has raised Him from the dead, you will be saved. For with the heart one believes unto righteousness, and with the mouth confession is made unto salvation. For the Scripture says, 'Whoever believes on Him will not be put to shame.' For there is no distinction between Jew and Greek, for the same Lord over all is rich to all who call upon Him. For 'whoever calls on the name of the Lord shall be saved.'" (Romans 10:9-13)

During the early years of marriage, we also started a business. We had a vision to start a craft supply store. We made contact with a man with whom I had grown up, who had a very profitable and successful store of this nature. Instead of coming out of that meeting encouraged, disappointment was all over the two of us. He knew we were regular customers, and he did not want to lose us. The picture he painted for us was one of impossibility with the limited resources we had. "There's got to be a way," we thought. We were not going to be defeated before we gave it our best shot. So with only five hundred dollars, we started our first business venture. Our newly-remodeled two-car garage became the home of Rinker's Handcrafts.

Did we have what my friend had in his shop? No. All the crafts we had were a handful of Styrofoam pieces and some felt squares, but our store was chucked full of candles, candle holders, ceramic pieces, candle arrangements, along with handmade marble lamps and other handmade items.

Business was very slow at the start, as the store was located in the country, seven miles from the nearest town. Advertising was very costly, so we came up with a plan. If people won't come to our store, then we will go to them. "Rinker's Home Show Party Plan" was our next move. A few contacts were made, one being to my sister and the other to my wife's aunt, and with these two bookings, we were off and running.

The parties were designed and set up this way: the hostess would invite friends, neighbors, and relatives into her home to view our merchandise which would be neatly arranged to attract attention, hopefully generating a sale. We would talk about each piece, give ideas on how they could personalize them into their own home décor, and then give them the opportunity to purchase these items. An incentive for the hostess was implemented whereby they would get a credit, a percentage of the sales for that evening with which they could purchase items of their choice. The hostess also received credit for any future bookings that they would generate.

It was an overnight success as we had many more bookings from these first two contacts, so many that I couldn't handle more, as I was out on these demonstrations five nights per week and still working a full time job. Growth came so rapidly that within a few months, we had hired and trained four additional people as demonstrators.

The cash flow we generated from these sales allowed us to expand our craft retail business and eventually start a second store. My wife, Nancy, managed the business and at times would be asked to speak and give demonstrations of items we sold in our store.

On one occasion she was asked to demonstrate bow-making at Christian Women's Club meeting. Immediately following this meeting, she started doing some things that were strange to me. I would find her praying and even talking out loud to the Lord. God had spared her life. At the age of twenty-four, doctors had discovered suspicious tissue on her womb, and she had to have a hysterectomy. What did God have or want from this woman?

I continued watching her. She was changing, and I wanted to know, what was up. What was going on that I didn't know about? Time would reveal a decision she had made, a decision to receive Jesus Christ into her life.

Hard work was paying off once again. Life was treating us great. We were making money and enjoying every minute of it.

"Trust in the Lord with all your heart, and lean not on your own understanding: In all ways acknowledge Him, and He shall direct your paths." (Proverbs 3:5-6)

Slowly things began to change. Things were happening that were out-of-control. I could feel a squeeze or pressure starting to build. Our demonstrators were beginning to find fault and not keeping the commitments they had made. The only positive thing I could see at this point in time was that Nancy was spending more and more time praying, talking to God.

Questions Only You Can Answer

Chapter 6 "On the Road to a New Beginning"

Can you name a time and place when you asked a friend for advice and because of their insecurity, they exaggerated in their response?

How damaging was this to your ego?

Have you ever witnessed a dramatic change in someone's life who is very dear and near to you, not knowing Romans 10:9-10 was the reason for this change?

What is the one thing that you will never forget about that change?

If, at this very moment in time, God were to grant you one desire of yours, what would it be?

What price would you willing to pay for this desire to be met?

Chapter 7

On the Road to a Business Failure

"Commit your works to the Lord, and your thoughts will be established." (Proverbs 16:3)

"A man's heart plans his way, but the Lord directs his steps." (Proverbs 16:9)

What was wrong with these two verses of scripture? Why were things not going in the direction we had planned? Does it not say in **Matthew 28:20, "... and lo, I am with you always, even to the end of the age"?**

After years of frivolous spending, I found that we were on an all too familiar road. We were "on the road to a business failure." Good credit had allowed us to buy many things, such as a box van to transport items, a motor home, a new quad-cab pick-up truck, a fifth-wheel camper, snowmobiles, motor cycles, all of which came with a payment book. I had reached the point where pressures from vendors demanding payments on past due accounts had me stressed to the point of thinking of a way out.

It was so bad that I began hearing voices saying, "Roger, you can get out of all this if you just follow my instructions.

Read your life insurance policy, page so and so, line so and so, and you will see that accidental death pays double indemnity." It was there in black and white, just as the voice had been saying. I read it for myself.

"Be sober, be vigilant; because your adversary the devil walks about like a roaring lion, seeking whom he may devour." (I Peter 5:8)

I had left a door open, and Satan had devised a plan for me to get out of the situation I was facing. The plan was laid out before me just like a blueprint. It was there, every detail which I needed for my way of escape, and yes, my wife would be financially secure.

Here was the plan, nothing too hard or complicated to follow: simply get into my car, drive only a mile, and there was a two-inch by six-inch piece of wood being supported across the road. This was placed there as a warning of a dead end caused by a newly constructed water reservoir. Simply crash through this barricade, drop into the deep water, and since this would be an accidental death, double indemnity would be Nancy's reward. That's it. Nothing could go wrong. No one would ever know the truth. A foolproof plan had been designed just for me.

The night had finally arrived. After closing the store, I sat in my office and once again reviewed and rehearsed the plan. This is it. Tonight's the night. No more pressure, no more having to make up excuses or stories as to when the check was put into the mail. Freedom was staring me in the eye.

After walking next door to our home, to which the business was attached, I kissed my already-sleeping wife and boys and said my final good-bye. None of them ever heard a word I had to say since they were sound asleep .

Once again I heard a voice, "Don't worry, they will be taken care of. This is your only way out." I climbed behind the wheel of our car. With the engine running, I pulled the lever into drive, and I was on my way. Only one mile to go, then a half mile as I rounded the final curve. I could see the board. I was almost there.

All of a sudden something snapped inside me. I heard a voice speaking to me. I slammed on the brakes. "What is it?" I said to myself. "What was that?"

"For God so loved the world that He gave His only begotten Son, that whoever believes in Him should not perish but have everlasting life." (John 3:16)

"Perish." Over and over, I kept hearing this word. I was about to perish. No, this cannot be! I have been deceived, I thought. I must return home and face reality. Once again I was reminded of the words my father spoke to me as a child, "Don't lie 'cuz' I'll find out the truth."

What transpired in the next couple of hours was one of the most difficult times of my life. I had to tell my wife the truth, because she needed to know. My mind was racing as I made the drive back home. I had to wake her from her sleep, not waiting for the morning. I had to tell her right away. How would she handle the news that we were deeply in debt and about to lose everything, our home and business and all of our toys?

You might think or wonder; didn't she know what was going on? Couldn't she see from the checkbook where we stood financially? No. She did not know for I had kept two sets of records. It had gotten so bad that I had even fixed the phones only to ring when I was standing next to them, so I was sure to answer all incoming calls.

I will never forget that night. My pride had to be broken. I had to admit failure and ask for Nancy's forgiveness, all very difficult things for me to do. She had every right to completely turn her back on me and call it quits, but instead she turned to me and said, "Hon, we will work it out somehow." After this, more than ever, I would find her on her knees, praying and talking to God. We made some necessary changes in the business, and we began opening Sundays at noon which allowed us time to start attending church.

Questions Only You Can Answer

Chapter 7 "On the Road to a Business Failure"

How do you define success?

Have you ever stepped out of your comfort-zone and decided to start a business venture?

Is frivolous spending, spending beyond your means, backing you into a corner?

Do you have a hard time discerning the voice of the Lord?

Are you totally convinced the Lord is always by your side, or do you experience times of feeling all alone?

What significance does the word "perish" have in your life?

Have you ever had to give up all you owned in order to survive?

Chapter 8

On the Road to Man's Failure

"Then Saul, still breathing threats and murder
against the disciples of the Lord, went to the high
priest and asked letters from him to the synagogues of Damascus, so that if he found any who
were of the Way, whether men or women, he might
bring them bound to Jerusalem. As he journeyed
he came near Damascus, and suddenly a light
shone around him from heaven. Then he fell to the
ground, and hearing a voice from heaven saying to
him, 'Saul, Saul, why are you persecuting Me?'"
(Acts 9:1-4)

Here was this man, Saul, who was a highly learned,
intelligent man who had a problem. He hated anyone
who was of the Way, which meant he disliked anyone who
believed in Christ. He was so determined to stop Christianity
that he had papers giving him the authority to capture men or
women who believed in Christ and to put them into bondage.
Saul was the type of person you hoped you would not have
an encounter with, that was before he came face to face with
Jesus Christ.

51

I had a problem with being a failure in business. I kept blaming myself for the way things were going and the direction things had taken. Then it happened. I heard a voice which I knew I had heard before. It was as clear as clear could be. This is what I heard:

"So God created man in His own image; in the image of God He created him; male and female He created them." (Genesis 1:27)

"My Son, your business may have failed, but I have never made a mistake. You are not a failure."

Could my past be forgiven just like God did for Saul? What was it going to take to turn me into a new creation, to be just like Him? During our years of operating the craft business which we had established, there were people with different dispositions who would visit the shop. One of these was a couple who would come and buy needlepoint kits. They were very friendly and would always want to talk. We knew very little about this couple other than the wife was a nurse. We knew where they lived, but we knew nothing about the man. That was until one day a comment was made about how she found time to do needlepoint, since we knew she had a very busy schedule. It was then we were informed that it was her husband who did the needlepoint, and not her. This man was different.

Periodically, they would stop at the shop, and the conversations became more interesting. One day as they were ready to leave the shop, the man reached into his pocket and handed Nancy a business card and said, "I would love for you and Roger to look me up sometime." To our surprise this man was an ordained pastor of a local church. Since we had changed our opening times on Sundays, we had put ourselves in a position that, if we wanted, we could attend some church services. The decision was made that it was time to go and visit this pastor's church.

As we arrived at the church, it seemed strange that the choir was already singing. It was thirty minutes until the service was to start or at least that's what we thought. We assumed that all church services started on the hour.

The words I had heard as a child began to well up inside me, "Don't ever be late for a meal or a meeting." Putting the flesh aside, we walked into the sanctuary and found the nearest seat.

As the pastor was speaking, he was standing at a podium to the left from where I sat. He was giving instructions as to the meaning of Holy Communion, and he said that the table had been prepared for us. He said, "Look," and for me to do so, I had to shift my eyes to the center of the altar where the actual table had been placed. As my eyes made the shift, I saw a vision of Christ standing there. His arms were outstretched, and He was reaching toward me. I never saw His face, only His body from the neck down, but I knew it was an invitation meant for me.

That day I decided that my life was not a failure, but that I was special in the eyes of God as He had extended a hand to me.

Questions Only You Can Answer

Chapter 8 "On the Road to Man's Failure"

Has there ever been a "Saul on the road to Damascus" experience in your life?

If so, who was your Ananias?

Do you struggle with blaming yourself for past failures in your life?

If so, how long do you suppose it will take you to let go and truly turn it over to God?

Do you believe God is bigger than anything you struggle with?

Do you truly believe that: God never made a mistake, we are not failures, and that we have been made in His image?

Have you ever heard the Lord speak directly to you in a voice unmistakably His?

Chapter 9

On the Road to the Big Decision

"But you are a chosen generation, a royal priesthood, a holy nation, His own special people, that you may proclaim the praises of Him who called you out of darkness into His marvelous light." (I Peter 2:9)

"That's me," I thought. "I am a chosen person. I have been chosen by God."

What was going on inside me? I could hardly wait for the next Sunday service. Every message I heard was as though the pastor were pointing his finger directly at me. When this happened I actually had problems breathing, and I thought I could not sit there and listen to any more of what was being spoken.

Then it finally happened. It was as though someone carried me to the altar. My feet and legs wanted to go the opposite direction, yet I was being carried to the altar. What was this I was experiencing? I was a person who always wanted to be in control of myself. I felt helplessly out-of-control. What was happening? What is this heaven-or-hell-thing this man of God is talking about? He has no knowledge of my past or present life style, so how can he dare to say that if I make a confession before God, He will forgive me of all my sins?

"That if you confess with your mouth the Lord Jesus and believe in your heart that God has raised Him from the dead, you will be saved. For with the heart one believes unto righteousness, and with the mouth confession is made unto salvation. For the Scripture says: 'Whoever believes on Him will not be put to shame.' For there is no distinction between Jew and Greek, for the same Lord over all is rich to all who call upon Him. For 'whoever calls on the name of the Lord shall be saved.'"
(Romans 10:9-13)

I began to ask God the question, "Is this what happened to my wife? Is this the reason why I find her on her knees talking to You so often?"

"... Most assuredly, I say to you, unless one is born again, he cannot see the kingdom of God."
(John 3:3)

I was trying desperately to yell, "Stop!" but the words would not come forth. I was being caught up into what seemed like a whirlwind. I was losing my composure. My mind kept on going back to all the things I had been taught and the things I had heard throughout the years. I had been to many services and had heard about God and Jesus, but what was this thing about being born-again? I was born once. That is how I came into the world, I thought. Now he is telling me I need to be born-again. Was this man for real? Did he know something I didn't? And this thing about confession, what is he saying? The only confession I had ever heard about was from my Catholic friends. I heard the stories as to how they had to go into a small booth and talk through a opening to someone sitting in a room next to them. Was God in the box, and were they making confession to Him?

For a moment I began to wonder, if I do make a confession, what will happen if I sin again? Many times my friends went to confession and then came back and partied and cussed and carried on just like before they went. So what sense is there in all this, I thought.

A flash went through my mind as I began asking myself this question, "What are all my friends going to think or say when they hear about this?"

Another chill went through my body as I remembered the story about Saul on the road to Damascus. He was actually imprisoning and killing people who believed in Jesus. Thank God, I thought, that is not where I am. I have not laid a hand on a person, and the only people whom my decisions effect are my family and myself. But then I was reminded about the rest of the story, and how he became blind for three days, and how Ananias was instructed to go to the home where Saul was staying. It was when this happened, that Saul had to trust in someone to lead him to his *destiny*, knowing that Ananias knew of his past actions, and how easy it would be for Ananias to take advantage of the situation.

How crazy I thought. The pastor was telling me all I needed to do to be born-again was to publicly confess Jesus as my Lord and Savior. Right there at that very moment, if I wanted to see the kingdom of heaven, because tomorrow might be too late. I felt like I had been hanging onto a stick suspended from a cliff, and my sweaty hands were beginning to loose their grip. Do not let go, do not let go, my mind was telling me. Hold on, or you will lose your self-control.

As I listened once again to the words being spoken, "God loves You, and He wants to have a relationship with you," my heart finally broke, as I lost my grip on pride.

What followed was like a tidal wave which carried me to the front of the church and the entire congregation, as these words came forth from my mouth, "I publicly declared that I had sinned, and I asked God to forgive me and for Jesus to come into my life and make me a new person."

Thank God, he had placed an Ananias in my life who obeyed his calling and was where God had wanted him to be at that time. That was the time He had preordained for me to receive Jesus Christ as my Savior.

Ananias was used by God to free Saul from bondage and set him on his road to recovery. As Ananias laid hands on him, he was, **"... filled with the Holy Spirit. Immediately there fell from his eyes something like scales, and he received his sight at once; and he arose and was baptized." (Acts 9:17b-18)**

I praise God for receiving my sight that day. I had been blind to the truth of His Word, but then I could see clearly. I was water baptized within a few weeks, and I started building a relationship with Him that day which continues growing stronger day by day.

"So then faith comes by hearing, and hearing by the word of God." (Romans 10:17)

Since my ears had been in tune with the things of the world, I asked God to switch channels for me. As He did, He filtered out the distractions of the world, and His word became clearer and clearer to me.

I had developed an extreme case of the "gimmies." Lord, give me more. I wanted all I could get my hands onto. I started attending classes and doing something I had never done before: reading His Word. Although there were many things I was reading that I did not comprehend, I continued reading, studying, and applying those truths to my life. It felt as though a ton of bricks had been removed from my body, and once again I could breath normally.

"The steps of a good man are ordered by the Lord, and He delights in his way." (Psalm 37:23)

I knew I was headed in the right direction as I was "on the road to recovery," having just made "The Big Decision."

uestions Only You Can Answer

Chapter 9 "On the Road to the Big Decision"

Do you see yourself as a special person, chosen by God, worthy to be called His son or daughter?

Have you ever experienced an out-of-control time in your life when you were being drawn into His marvelous light?

Have you ever made a confession according to Romans 10:9-10 about your life?

Do you believe we will spend eternity in one of two places, either with Him in heaven or forever separated from Him in hell?

Are you assured that if you were to die this day, you would see the kingdom of God as recorded in John 3:3?

If you did not answer "yes" to the questions concerning Romans 10:9-10 and John 3-3, what is standing in your way?

If all roads lead somewhere, where do you think the road on which you are now traveling will eventually lead you?

Do you feel something tugging at your heart this very moment, and you know it is God beckoning to you?

If so, why not make one of the biggest decisions you will ever have to make, and ask Jesus into your heart?

Do you realize it doesn't matter where you may be reading this book, in the privacy of your home, or on lunch-break at work, or wherever you are, you can ask Him to forgive you of your sins and He will?

Why not make this day your day of "A New Birth, A New Beginning," simply by praying this prayer:

"Lord, I admit to You that I have sinned and fallen short of Your glory. Forgive me, cleanse me and make me a new creation in You. I confess with my mouth, the Lord Jesus, and believe in my heart that You raised Him from the dead and by doing so I am saved, I am a born-again child of Yours. Thank you, Lord, for rescuing me from the pit of hell. Amen."

It is my sole intent of writing this book to make people conscious of the fact that life is a journey, and we will spend eternity either in heaven or in hell. The choice is entirely up to each of us.

If you have just prayed this simple prayer for the first time, may I be the first to congratulate you and welcome you as a fellow brother or sister in Christ.

Now let me encourage you to go and share the good news with others. It is your testimony as to what God has done for you. I would love to hear from you as well. I can be contacted at the information found on the inside of the back cover of this book

Chapter 10

On the Road to Recovery - Letting Go of the Past

"The word which came to Jeremiah from the Lord, saying: 'Arise and go down to the potter's house, and there I will cause you to hear My words.' Then I went down to the potter's house, and there he was, making something at the wheel. And the vessel that he made of clay was marred in the hand of the potter; so he made it again into another vessel, as it seemed good to the potter to make." (Jeremiah 18:1-4)

Mary Magdalene was a young woman who had a past she would have liked to forget. She was a prostitute. She had sold her body, and men paid for her love. The Pharisees, as recorded in Luke 7, called her "an especially wicked sinner." She did have a past, one you would not get excited about and want to share with everyone. Truly her past was one worth running from. Mary had an ugly past, but through Jesus, she had a beautiful future. In fact, Jesus forgave her of her sins, and Mary, in return wanted to show her love and appreciation.

In Luke 7:36-50 we read the account of another Mary anointing Jesus' feet with very expensive perfume, then washing them with her tears and drying them with her hair. What she did was condemned by many people, simply because of her past, but truly it was an act of true love and honor.

Saul (Paul) had a past record as well and would have liked to have it removed from the minds of people. Many people remembered him as the person who persecuted Christians. How could this man possibly be used by God? Did God forget what Saul had done? In spite of his past, he became the apostle who recorded two-thirds of the New Testament by direct revelation from God Himself.

"If we confess our sins, He is faithful and just to forgive us of our sins and to cleanse us from all unrighteousness." (I John 1:9)

After reading about Mary Magdalene and Paul, only two of the many whose lives were transformed, we realize that God does not remember our pasts. Because of the decision I made that day, my past became my past. By my confession and the belief in my heart, I was cleansed. I had a choice to make and that was to let go and move onward and upward or to remain in bondage.

For all those years, I had a huge void in my life. Now the void was being filled with Jesus. My life had taken a new direction. I was falling deeper and deeper in love with Jesus. Immediately after asking Jesus into my life, I was encouraged to be water-baptized. Why, I asked, for I knew as an infant my parents had me sprinkle-baptized, as was the custom of the church they were attending. Why was it of so much a concern that immersion was being suggested?

I was searching for the truth, and the truth was about to be revealed. I was encouraged to read John 1:19-34, which I did. Jesus Himself was baptized as an adult, and when He came up out of the water, John records in verse 32, "**... I saw the Spirit descending from heaven like a dove, and He remained upon Him.**" As I read this, my heart began to leap for joy. Yes, that's what I wanted. I wanted to be more like Jesus.

When the day came, and I was baptized, I knew that I had done what Jesus did, and He was well-pleased with me. As the Holy Spirit came upon me, He left me in a state of wanting more of Him and less of myself. I began to saturate myself with the Word of God and started attending new believers' classes.

"But as many as received Him, to them He gave the right to become children of God, to those who believed in His name." (John 1:12)

Receiving Him as I did and believing in His name, I began to realize as a child of God, I had rights I never had before.

"For by grace you have been saved through faith, and that not of yourselves; it is the gift of God." (Ephesians 2:8)

What a gift I had just received, eternal life, and I knew where I would spend eternity.

"Casting all your care upon Him for He cares for you." (I Peter 5:7)

There was no need to carry my burdens any longer. He was there for me. I was no longer alone and having to do things by my own abilities, because now God was my strength. My life had been totally transformed, by the Potter's mighty hand. He took the marred, cracked, out-of-shape me and was now reshaping me. This did not happen overnight or without times of having my faith tested.

We still had our business, and vendors were still waiting on what was due them. But now God was on our side. Somehow, between God and us, we would work things out this time. Phoning all our suppliers and explaining our situation was the first step. All agreed, something, no matter how large or small the amount of the check, was better than nothing at all. We were sincere about paying off our debts. Rather than our declaring bankruptcy, which would mean that they would get nothing, again they all agreed to continue selling to us, but this time on a cash-only delivery basis.

We had put the business up for sale, but had no buyers. It seemed a home and business all in one came with too large a price tag. That was until one day God sent the right person, a Christian Brother who immediately purchased the home and business.

"Now faith is the substance of things hoped for, the evidence of things not seen." (Hebrews 11:1)

"So then faith cometh by hearing, and hearing by the word of God." (Romans 10:17)

Our faith in the Word of God carried us through this period of time. We kept believing, not always seeing, but having confidence in the unseen until it became a reality. We were "on the road to recovery."

Questions Only You Can Answer

Chapter 10 "On the Road to Recovery - Letting Go of the Past"

Are you in need of a make-over?

Are you looking at a clean slate in reference to your life?

Do you feel you are a righteous person?

Have you been water-baptized as a person capable of making your own decisions?

Do you totally understand your rights as a child of God?

Have you reached the point of casting all your cares upon Him, not holding anything back?

Do you have a problem with believing "that faith is the substance of things hoped for, the evidence of things not seen"?

Are you a "seeing-is-believing" type person?

Chapter 11

On the Road to Stepping Out - Our First Missionary Trip

"The steps of a good man are ordered by the Lord, and He delights in his way. Though he fall, he shall not be utterly cast down: for the Lord upholds him with His hand." (Psalm 37:23-24)

I knew beyond any reasonable doubt the Lord had rescued me, and now was ordering my footsteps. But where do I go from here? How is His plan for my life going to be revealed to me?

"For I know the thoughts that I think toward you, says the Lord, thoughts of peace and not of evil, to give you a future and a hope. Then you will call upon Me and go and pray to Me, and I will listen to you. And you will seek Me and find Me, when you search for Me with all your heart." (Jeremiah 29:11-13)

"The Lord will perfect that which concerns me..." (Psalm 138:8a)

"Being confident of this very thing, that He who has begun a good work in you will complete it until the day of Jesus Christ." (Philippians 1:6)

Knowing that God had a plan for my life was exciting. But exactly what was it, and how would I accomplish His purpose for my life? "Get involved, do something," my heart was saying, "just as you did when you first started a business. If people will not come to you, go to them." Get involved I did, volunteering to be a greeter and usher, my first responsibilities of involvement in a church. I could hardly wait for a Sunday morning, wanting to be the first one there, so I could welcome others into the house of the Lord. I knew the importance of a warm welcome.

My first visit to that church in Cherryville, Pennsylvania, was one I will never forget. That particular Sunday, as I walked up to the main entrance, the moment I stepped up to that door, it swung wide open and out came a hand extended toward me. There stood a giant of a man who made me feel welcome. That greeting and welcome made a lasting impression in my life, so that I wanted to do the same for others. Every Sunday we were there, Nancy and I, greeting all who came to the house of the Lord. Take note I did say, "we", as "we" were both committed. Every time we heard volunteers were needed, we were there. Building scenes for the annual Christmas outreach or working with the adult choir to raise funds for the purchase of new choir gowns. We volunteered to travel with the youth on a choir tour throughout Florida. We also got involved in fund-raising projects for mission outreaches.

What a joy it was serving the Lord. The road was wide, but now I sensed the path becoming smaller, more narrow as I reread the scripture in **Psalm 138:8, "The Lord will perfect that which concerns me."**

We became heavily involved in missions fund-raising. It was exciting, but also challenging. It appeared that some people did a lot of talking, but when it was time for them to put their words into action, they somehow were among the missing.

"Get over it," I was told. "Man will fail you, but never God. Keep your eyes on God and not on man," was the advice given to me.

Something was stirring inside me. I kept feeling like God wanted me to go to the mission field. That feeling was constantly there and would not go away. "Okay, okay," I thought, "this is it. I'm giving in. No more excuses, Lord. I will go!" I reasoned to myself, "There's plenty of time to change my mind as the next planned outreach was over a year away. Maybe, just maybe, God will forget about it and let me off the hook."

It was at this time in my life that I had given up working road construction. Tired of always being away from home, I had found a job working with a local excavating contractor. I recall coming home one night and finding my wife in a state of excitement. I had never seen her like this before, not the normal, "How was your day, and are you ready to eat?" but she greeted me carrying a section of a local newspaper.

What is this all about? What has her so excited? What's on sale that I need to know about? I was about to find out what she had in her hand. She was carrying an ad about an evangelist who was coming into a neighboring city. He had scheduled fourteen nights of meetings, and they were to be held in a tent. She said, "I know this is going to be great. We need to go, and I am telling every one I know that they should go as well."

By now my stomach was growling. It wanted food, and her actions did not lead me to believe any food was going to be served, not at that moment. Not only was I hungry and tired, but now anger welled up in me, and I yelled, "Stop! Nancy, you know nothing about this evangelist, his ministry, what he believes in, or what he preaches about, and here you are telling others that they need to go to these meetings!"

Her response to all this was, "I feel something inside me, and it feels good about these meetings." Reluctantly I gave in and said I would go to one meeting. I wanted to keep peace in the family. However, it didn't end with one, as we attended thirteen of the fourteen nights of meetings.

This evangelist was different. He spoke in a language to which I could relate. I had heard some speakers before who used words I had no understanding of, or I couldn't figure out what the point was that they were trying to make. Somehow I had connected with this man and the ministry he ran called "Christ is the Answer."

It was on the last night, that he gave an altar call that would change our lives forever. This was the question he presented to all in attendance, "Are you ready to respond 'yes' to God, that you will go wherever He wants you to go, and you will do whatever He wants you to do?" Now that stopped me in my tracks. My heart was thumping out-of-control as we, hand in hand, made our way to the altar.

The next words I heard the man of God say were these, "This is not a time of fun and games, but a very serious time. You are about to say 'yes' to God that you will go wherever and do whatever He asks of you. Now if you don't feel comfortable with this decision, then go back to your seats and be seated. No one will think anything less of you; at least you are being honest with yourself and with God." I recall looking at my wife, and as I did, she said, "We are going to do it. Tonight is our night." Humbly we got on our knees and committed our lives to the Lord. No doubts, no reservations, no plea bargaining, just a simple "yes" with child-like faith.

That night did not end with our being released to go back to our seats as normal. This was just the beginning. At the conclusion of the service, the evangelist walked up to me and said, "I want to extend an invitation to you and your wife to join me on a mission outreach to India."

How could this be? We had just made a commitment to the Lord to go wherever or do whatever He wanted, and within minutes we were being asked to go to India. "Lord, is this for real, and am I hearing his man correctly? He did say India, did he not? Is this what the scriptures mean as stated in **Mark 16:15?**"

"And He said to them, 'Go into all the world and preach the gospel to every creature.'"

I stood speechless, grasping for something to say. I felt like a boxer who had just taken a punch, knocking the wind out of me. As I gained my composure, I knew I needed to ask some questions, like, "When will this outreach take place, and how much will all this cost?

His reply to my questions was simply this, "We will be leaving in two weeks. The cost will be about 15 hundred dollars per person. Here is a phone number you will need to call, and I will see you in New York in two weeks." End of conversation.

My first thoughts were, "There is no way. There is no way I am going to take all the money we have in the bank, 3 thousand dollars, and spend it on a trip to India. Surely this was not from the Lord, because He knows how hard I have worked for this money, and surely He wouldn't ask us to make such a sacrifice."

On the drive home I don't recall if many words were spoken as we were both is a state of shock. I prayed, "Lord, please cut me a break and give me some time to get my head cleared up?"

A day later, my wife had invited a future bride-to-be to our home along with her fiancé. She was going to be making their wedding flower arrangements. As the evening progressed, this young man and I moved to our kitchen where we were about to engage in some man-to-man talk. In the course of the conversation I mentioned about the previous night and what had happened. I recall his turning and looking directly into my eyes and saying, "Well, Roger, are you going to be disobedient again?"

How rude of this young man to say such a thing to me! How dare he speak to me as if I were being disobedient! He was not a stranger to me as I not only knew him, but I knew his family as well, and had spent time with him before. His words went deep into my soul, as I knew he was speaking the truth, and I responded with, "Troy, shut-up!"

Within minutes after their departure, I was in search of the piece of paper upon which was written the phone number I had been given by the evangelist. Something inside me was telling me to get in contact with this person. I had no idea where I was calling or to whom I would be speaking as I dialed the number.

One ring, then two and three and so on, and no one answered. "That's it. I am off the hook. At least I tried to make contact." Off to bed we go as I had to get some rest, because the next day was a workday for me.

"Rest in the Lord, and wait patiently for Him..." (Psalm 37:7)

All night long I tossed and turned as rest would not come. I felt dirty inside, confused, and tormented by what had been spoken to me. As the alarm went off, I jumped out of bed and got ready to leave for work. Before leaving the house, I went to our bedroom to give my wife a kiss. I then very softly said to her, "I'm going to give that number another try today."

Not knowing if she heard me or not, I did hear her mumble something from under the covers which by now had been pulled up over her head.

At our nine o'clock morning break-time, I headed to the nearest pay phone. (This was before cell phones.) My hands were quivering as I tried to insert the money into the slot, and nervously I dialed the number.

One ring, and then two, and then I hear a voice saying, "Hello, this is ... " She gave her name and the name of the travel agency she was employed by. My heart stopped as I heard this woman speaking, and then she asked me how she could be of assistance. I explained to her that I was given this number by an evangelist whom we had met, and that it concerned a trip he was making to India in two weeks. She acknowledged she knew this man and asked again how she could be of assistance.

My response was this, "Do you know if there would possibly be two more seats available on that flight?" This was the time before computers were at everyone's fingertips. She informed me that she would check and get back to me as soon as possible. She added that the possibility of getting tickets, because of such a short notice, were slim. When I heard the word "slim," I gave another sigh of relief. I had made another attempt and felt once again as if I was off the hook.

Before ending the conversation with this woman, I informed her that, when she did have an answer, she should call my wife. She was working in a church office and could be reached by phone, whereas I could not. Later that day, Nancy did receive a phone call from the travel agent. The phone call went something like this: "Mrs Rinker, I have good news for you. I have checked, and you and your husband are going to India in ten days."

This good news came as a shock, as Nancy did not even know prior to her receiving the call, that I had contacted the travel agency. I recall coming home that night and finding my wife in a state of shock mixed with excitement. I had never seen her this way before. It was not the normal, "How was your day, and are you ready to eat?" Instead she greeted me, this time not carrying a section of a local newspaper, but with the words, "Guess what happened to me today? I received a phone call - and we are going to India."

Here it was. We had made a commitment to the Lord, and supernaturally He arranged for two open seats on a flight leaving in ten days at the same price of those booked weeks prior.

My next step was to call my boss and inform him of my need for three weeks off. Plus, I would need the following day off, as I had to travel to New York to obtain our visas. Breaking the news to him was no problem as he was a brother in the Lord and totally understood the challenges we were facing.

Off to New York I went and spent an entire day there, until I was able to secure our visas.

The day of departure came and another brother in the Lord drove us to JFK airport in New York City, where we were to meet the evangelist. Upon checking in, we headed directly to the waiting area at the gate from which we would be leaving. This is where we were to meet the evangelist. Departure time was rapidly approaching, and we could not find this man. The final boarding call was announced, and still there was no sign of the evangelist. By now Nancy was in a state of panic.

We had made it this far and had only limited information of where we were going, other than to India and then Italy. We had no knowledge of where we would be staying, or who would be meeting us from the group once we arrived in India. We were walking by faith, and our faith was presently on shifting sand.

Looking around in desperation we saw a young woman named April, whom we had met at the tent crusade. She was also going on the same trip, but she only had a one way ticket. We asked her, "Have you seen the evangelist?" She replied "yes" and instructed us to get on the plane. We were also informed that the evangelist and his son were having diffi-culties boarding due to the large number of cameras, battery packs, and recording devices they were carrying.

It was at this time Nancy informed me that she would board, but there were conditions. If the evangelist were unable to board the flight, once we reached England, where we had to change planes, we would be on the next fight back to the United States.

We found our seats and began to prepare ourselves for take off. As the captain of the airplane began to make an announcement for the flight attendants to prepare for take off, we heard a loud commotion happening at the doorway to the plane. All eyes were focused on this area wondering what was going on. Who walked in, but this blond-haired Texan evangelist, who stood six-foot seven-inches tall! There was no mistaking him. This was the man who was holding up the plane's departure. We both gave a big sigh of relief as we now felt a little better, knowing he had made the flight.

Once arriving in England and departing from the airplane, we were escorted into a holding area where we would be spending the next couple of hours. It was there we finally were able to talk to the evangelist. He informed us that, due to the large number of cameras, battery packs, and recording devices they were carrying, each of us would be responsible to carry some of the equipment for the remainder of the trip, to avoid additional clearance regulations.

While waiting for our next flight, we were informed that we must all go outside on the tarmac, claim and identify our luggage, and hand carry it through customs. This was a first for us. Once outside, we saw our luggage scattered all over the ground. Gathering all our luggage, we got in line to go through customs. At that point we not only had to give account for what we had in our luggage, but we were being questioned about the video/recording equipment we were carrying.

This evangelist had a way with people. As these agents were questioning us, he was standing there saying, "Just pass through. It's okay," and pass through we did.

Finally, we were airborne once again heading to India. Arriving in Bombay, India was a sight we were not ready for. It was as we departed from the airplane that we saw military men armed with machine guns in a ready position. They were everywhere. What a welcome sight! What had we gotten ourselves into?

We all made our way through customs, that is all except the evangelist. He was being detained, because of the equipment he was carrying. The rest of us decided we would not wait for him, but we would go and meet the missionary who had been waiting for our arrival.

Once in the lobby we were met by the leader of the group from "Christ is the Answer." What a welcome sight! He was an American whom we could understand. This man would be like a father to us for the next two weeks. He escorted us to a mini-bus, which would be our transportation. We loaded all our belongings and started the wait.

By now it was almost ten o'clock at night, and the temperature was still over a hundred degrees. An hour passed by and still there was no evangelist. Time was ticking away, and the missionary was getting nervous as midnight was rapidly approaching. He informed us that the more time we spent sitting there at the airport, the more dangerous it was getting.

After what seemed like an eternity, we saw the figure of a man emerging from the customs area. What a relief as we saw this tall Texan walking out of the airport with all his equipment!

We were heading north "on the road to" an eight hour journey to the place where we would be spending the next week. Driving in India is totally different than driving in the United States. First of all, they drive on the left hand side of the road, and they are constantly blowing their horns, and many people drive at night without their headlights on. It is also not uncommon for a driver, especially the driver of a large truck, of which there are many, to stop and park his vehicle on the highway, crawl under it and go to sleep.

The eight hour journey over bumpy roads was one that would create a problem for me as time progressed. I had had a back injury which required surgery. All the time I was sitting on the airplane and then on the mini-bus caused a disc to slip out of alignment. By the time we reached our destination, I was in misery.

We were shown where we were going to be staying. It was a home that normally was occupied by a doctor. It had a kitchen, bath, and several bedrooms. Homes in India, especially in the tribal country where we were, definitely were not like what we had been accustomed to living in our home country. The bedroom we were assigned to had nothing but a bed. We were fortunate, however, as some had to sleep on the floor on bamboo mats. The bathroom next door did have a toilet to sit on, a bowl, and a tub. The tub had no running water. You had to use water from a bucket and a ladle when bathing, and NO hot water. The bathroom was connected to a sewer line to get rid of the waste. However, it ended two feet outside the wall. When being used, it dumped everything on the ground. This was next to our bedroom window! They say home is where you hang your hat. This was where we were about to hang our hats.

It was from here that we traveled out to different areas where we were involved in daytime ministry and nighttime crusades. It was from here, where I would be able to walk to a hospital to seek medical assistance for my aching back. I had no choice. I needed medical attention, and I had been told of a man who could help me.

So we went to the hospital, Nancy by my side as usual. It was only a short walk and having been given instructions as to where to go, that was the direction in which we proceeded. This was a partially open-air hospital. One area we passed through had IV bottles just lying outside in the open. People were cooking over open fires, and everything was covered with dust and dirt.

Finally, we reached the door that led to the doctor's office. Upon knocking on the door and getting no response, we decided to go back the way we came and try another means of entrance.

What we saw next was a sight I had never seen before, and I pray I will never see again! There, lying on the path we had just moments before walked on, was this large green snake! This was inside the hospital compound! Could this be what they use when a person needs anesthesia? Do they just allow the snake to bite them? Needless to say, we did a 180 degree turn and proceeded in the opposite direction.

Using another approach, we did find the door leading to the doctor's office. Upon knocking and being told to enter, we once again are faced with a first. This time it was a doctor who was blind! I informed him that I had severe pain in my lower back. He then instructed me to remove my shirt, and he proceeded to examine me. As he ran his hands down my spine, he said, "Tell me about the surgery you had." My faith was now rising as this man could tell I had surgery, even though he was blind.

He then told me to lie on the table so he could adjust my back. After which He proceeded to give me a heat lamp treatment to remove the swelling. My thoughts were, "How is this man going to know if and when the skin on my back turns red, other than when he smells the flesh burning?"

No problem! This man's eyes were in his hands. Very gently he adjusted my back, getting the disc back into alignment, and treated the affected area. He also prescribed some medication, which I gladly accepted as I wanted to enjoy this time in India.

"On the Road to Ministry"

It was on one of these daytime ministry events that the group had gathered under a pavilion-type structure to minister the Word of God. I decided to walk off to the side and videotape part of the action. I was only a hundred feet from where the group was, standing on top of an embankment, minding my own business, shooting video. All of a sudden I heard some commotion coming from behind. I turned around to see what was happening. I did not understand what I was witnessing. Within seconds a mob of men had surrounded me!

I took notice that many of the men had something in their hands that looked like a clay jar, while others were holding something behind their backs. Not knowing what to think of all this or what to do, I stood still as two uniformed police men made their way through the mob. In broken English one of them said to me, "Who is this Jesus they are talking about? You better get out of here!"

My first response was, "I don't know this Jesus they are talking about. I'm only here to take video pictures." As I spoke these words I heard the sound of a rooster crowing. This was a lie. I was in fear of losing my life. I had been informed that two weeks prior to our arrival the people had captured a missionary and had him tied to the stake and had actually started a fire before letting him go.

After my response to the officer that I didn't know Jesus, he said something to the mob, and they gradually started to disperse. As soon as I saw an opening in the crowd, I made my way back to the rest of the group who had witnessed what had just happened.

Immediately, most of us boarded the mini-van, and we drove to the other end of the city in which we were ministering. Some of the more brave souls decided to walk, but not Nancy and me. Our security was in the mini-bus.

It was not until later on that I found out what the clay like looking jars contained and what some of the men were holding behind their backs, and why these men protested to our being at that certain location. First, we were in front of a Hindu school. Second, the men had acid in the clay jars which they would throw into a person's eyes, blinding them. Third, the others had lead pipes which they would then use to club a person to death.

"On the Road to the Other End of Town"

As we arrived at the other end of town, we asked the missionary if it were possible to get something to drink. He said we could, and he proceeded toward a small stand to purchase some sodas for all of us.

As he was out of the mini-bus making the purchase, I looked down a side street, and much to my disbelief came the same mob of men which I just had an encounter. We shouted for the missionary, and as he rushed back to the bus, those men had already hit one of the brothers on the head and had placed Hindu stickers all over the bus.

Finally, we made it back to where the group who were not staying with us, were camping. This happened to be an old Missionary Alliance camp, located only a few miles from where this incident happened. God's hand of protection was with us, as I'm quite sure everyone in town knew where we were staying.

The group continued ministering in nightly crusades held in an open field just outside of the city limits. People came by the hundreds, walking through grass fields infected with cobra snakes. Nothing was going to keep them from hearing the Word. Many people gave their lives to the Lord, and we witnessed miracle after miracle.

After completing our ministry time in this area of India, we headed back to Bombay for our journey to Italy. All the while these meetings were being held, I still had a back problem. In fact, the night we went to leave, I had gotten medicine from the doctor that totally knocked me out. I was completely out of it as far as what was going on all around us.

As the bus headed for Bombay, a group of motorcyclists decided they were going to torment our missionary friend. They would not let him pass as they kept zigzagging in front of the bus. This went on for hours.

Needless to say everything that had happened since we left the United States was playing heavily on my wife's mind. Not only was I unable to protect her, but she had to make sure all our belongings were being taken care of. At this point in time, I was being cautious not to lift or carry anything which might cause more injury to my back. That night there was another long eight hour trip, and although I was heavily sedated, my back continued to get worse.

Once we reached Bombay, Nancy and I decided it was best if we would return to the States and not continue on to Italy with the rest of the group. Knowing flight changes had to be made, the missionary immediately went to the airport and within a few minutes returned with our new tickets. We would be flying out in a couple of hours.

Looking back in time, I can now see where God's hand of protection was definitely with us as we made this journey, even though we did not realized that, **"'No weapon formed against you shall prosper, and every tongue which rises against you in judgment, you shall condemn. This is the heritage of the servants of the Lord, and their righteousness is from Me,' says the Lord." (Isaiah 54:17)**

Had I passed the test? Was God pleased with what had been accomplished, or would I be required to go back and make right those things in which I may have failed? Was this the one and only missionary trip that God wanted us to participate in? Or was this just one of the many "on the road to" journeys we would have to travel?

83

I had mentioned in the beginning of this chapter that when we were asked to go to India, that one of my first questions was, "How much is all this going to cost?" I was informed it would 3 thousand dollars for the both of us to go and that was all we had in our savings. We had used every penny we had, but when we returned, praise God, He had very graciously provided. He made provision through man, and it was through man that we had received back, every dollar we had spent.

Questions Only You Can Answer

Chapter 11 "On the Road to Stepping Out - Our First Missionary Trip"

Knowing that a good person's steps are ordered by God, have you struggled taking the first step with Him?

How confident are you when walking in the unknown?

Have you had to look for excuses for not doing exactly as the Lord has directed?

Have you ever found yourself in a life threatening situation?

Has anyone ever spoken a word into your life that you hated to hear, and yet you knew it was the truth?

Have you ever doubted God's plan for your life?

How do you think you would respond if asked the question, "Who is this Jesus they are talking about?" knowing your response could mean life or death?

Chapter 12

On the Road to Uncovering
Something Undone

After returning from India on our first mission experience, it was not long before something inside me started to surface once again. It was something I had tried to hide and put out of my mind concerning my involvement with a group going to Honduras. Regardless of how hard I tried to forget about this trip, I was failing. It became more and more vivid in my mind. It was all I could think about. I knew how God had miraculously saved me from disaster in India, and how He financially provided for our every need, but I still put up a wall of resistance. The words, "Oh, you of little faith" kept bombarding my mind. Why was I being tormented?

> **"By this we know love, because He laid down His life for us. And we also ought to lay down our lives for the brethren. But whoever has this world's goods, and sees his brother in need, and shuts up his heart from him, how does the love of God abide in him?" (I John 3:16-17)**

Where was my level of faith? Did I trust more in the goods of this world that I had acquired than I trusted in God? Was I following God's example of loving others? Was God's love truly abiding in me?

"Stop! Stop!" I cried. "Okay, I get the message. Lord, I will go!"

Within a few months after returning from India, we were headed to Honduras. There we would be working with a missionary whom our home church was supporting. This was going to be a work outreach. All of us on the team were very excited about going. We were informed that there would be times when we would be given the opportunity to share our testimonies. We worked on a church building, constructed walls for a radio broadcast studio, did electrical wiring and painting, and whatever was asked of us. We were there to serve.

In the evenings before we would go to a church service, the missionary couple would have us all gather for a time of reflection and a time for questions and answers. It was at one of these gatherings that the missionary made a statement that has remained with me to this day, "You cannot steer a parked car," and, "One must bloom where God has planted him."

Regarding the statement, "You cannot steer a parked car," I knew the concept of what he was referring to. Unless one puts himself into motion, he cannot be guided in any specific direction and will remain where he is. I understood that part.

However, "One must bloom where God has planted them," left me with questions. Exactly what was he referring to? I was informed that you have to take root, grow, and mature wherever God places you. "Wherever God places you." These words kept ringing in my ears. What impact could that possibly have on my life in the future?

We accomplished all we had planned and much more. We also experienced times when we were given the opportunity to share our personal testimonies. The fear of standing up in front of a group of people was diminishing. God had sent us there on a mission, and we were happy seeing things unfold before our eyes.

After completing our time in Honduras, we returned home and within the next year, we were headed back to the same place. Once again, we had a construction project as our main purpose. We were given the opportunity to share our testimonies, too. One day our mission leader asked if any of us minded going to work for a fellow missionary, although he was not part of our denomination. My wife and I, along with a few others, said yes, we would go and do whatever we could to help this family.

It was during the time we spent with this family that we, Nancy and I, noticed something different about this couple. In fact, we approached them and asked if we could have a private meeting with them. They graciously accepted our request.

What was it? Why were they so different? What did they have that we were sensing? Was there any way we too could have what they had? What was this void in our lives? Time would reveal the answers for which we were searching.

We asked them from which church that they had been commissioned and sent out on the mission field. They responded, "We are here as part of an outreach from a church located in Lancaster, Pennsylvania." How strange, we thought, that they were from a church that was less than two hours travel time from we were living. Our thoughts were that someday we will have to go and visit the church and possibly meet their pastor.

Shortly after arriving home, curiosity got the best of us, and we decided to go and visit the church in Lancaster. What was it this couple had, and could we possibly have the same thing?

"And being assembled together with them, He commanded them not to depart from Jerusalem, but to wait for the Promise of the Father, 'which,' He said, 'you have heard from Me; for John truly baptized with water, but you shall be baptized with the Holy Spirit not many days from now.'"
(Acts 1:4-5)

Was this the answer? Were they baptized with the Holy Spirit? Was that what was being revealed to us as missing in our lives? "Uncovering something undone" sent us on a journey, searching for the answers.

"But you shall receive power when the Holy Spirit has come upon you; and you shall be witnesses to Me in Jerusalem, and in all Judea and Samaria, and to the end of the earth." (Acts 1:8)

That was the answer. We had not been baptized with the Holy Spirit, and that was the void we were experiencing in our lives.

"And it shall come to pass in the last days, says God, that I will pour out of My Spirit on all flesh; your sons and your daughters shall prophesy, your young men shall see visions, your old men shall dream dreams. And on My menservants and on My maidservants I will pour out My Spirit in those days; and they shall prophesy."
(Acts 2:17-18)

Believing that we were living in the days being spoken of in the scriptures, we wanted that power. The wait was over. We asked to be baptized with His Holy Spirit, and we did receive.

Questions Only You Can Answer

Chapter 12 "On the Road to Uncovering Something Undone"

Do you have a problem with letting go of your earthly possessions?

Do you a problem with getting your priorities to line up with God's plan for your life?

Do you see yourself as a parked car?

Are there any signs of growth, or are you in a state of dormant, as to where you are planted, or have you not taken root yet?

Have you ever seen something in someone else's life that you desired in yours (such as the baptism of the Holy Spirit)?

Do you believe that we are living in the days spoken of in Acts 2:17?

If you have asked Jesus into your life, have you received the baptism of the Holy Spirit?

Chapter 13

On the Road to Facing
the Giants in Life

"Now the Philistines gathered their armies
together to battle, and were gathered at Sochoh,
which belongs to Judah; they encamped between
Sochoh and Azekah, in Ephes Dammim. And Saul
and the men of Israel were gathered together, and
they encamped in the Valley of Elah and drew
up in battle array against the Philistines. The
Philistines stood on a mountain on one side, and
Israel stood on a mountain on the other side, with
a valley between them.

And a champion went out from the camp of
the Philistines, named Goliath, from Gath, whose
height was six cubits and a span."
(I Samuel 17:1-4)

The Philistines had a giant of a man on their side. This
man was huge, standing almost 9-feet 9- inches tall. He
wore a helmet, a coat of armor weighing 126 pounds and
carried a spear weighing almost 16 pounds. He knew he was
big, and he also had a big mouth. He tantalized the Israelites

and put forth a challenge, **"Choose a man for yourselves and let him come down to me." (I Samuel 17:8b)**

He was looking for trouble and wanted to fight anyone who would stand up against him. He even made this statement,

"If he is able to fight with me and kill me, then we will be your servants. But if I prevail against him and kill him, then you shall be our servants and serve us." (I Samuel 17:9)

Goliath was confident in who he was. Nothing was going to stop him because of his size, strength, and the armor he carried. He challenged all men, "Come and do battle with me, and I will teach you a thing or two."

A young shepherd boy named David was about to teach him a significant lesson.

"Then David said to Saul, "Let no man's heart fail because of him; your servant will go and fight with this Philistine." (I Samuel 17:32)

David had confidence, too, but his confidence was in the name of the Lord of hosts. As a shepherd he had faced giants before: a lion and a bear, which were no match for him. So why should he be overly concerned with this giant of a man with a big mouth? Did the bear and lion not have big mouths as well?

As David was about to prepare for battle, King Saul had an idea of how David should dress. Saul wanted him to wear his armor suit, and David was about to tell Saul, "No, this is not for me. This is yours. This is what you wear for battle."

"... And David said to Saul, 'I cannot walk with these, for I have not tested them.' So David took them off." (I Samuel 17:39b)

David said something very important in that verse of scripture when he said, "For I have not tested them." Saul was asking him to use something with which he was not familiar. Many times we engage in a battle with something in our hand or clothed in something we have not tested, and then we wonder why our endeavors fail.

David dressed for battle.

"Then he took his staff in his hand; and he chose for himself five smooth stones from the brook, and put them in a shepherd's bag, in a pouch which he had, and his sling was in his hand. And he drew near to the Philistine." (I Samuel 17:40)

As David approached him, Goliath had a few more smart remarks to make, but David held his tongue.

"Then David said to the Philistine, 'You come to me with a sword, with a spear, and with a javelin. But I come to you in the name of the Lord of hosts, the God of the armies of Israel, whom you have defied.'" (I Samuel 17:45)

David had a coat of armor not visible by the human eye or human understanding. "In the name of the Lord" was his suit of armor. It was all he needed to defeat this Philistine.

Let me tell you about a real life giant with whom I came face to face.

A Provoked Man Decides to Do
An Extreme Make-Over on Me!

A working man, tired from a long day at work, arrived home to be met by his wife. This day she was so excited for his return that she met him in the driveway of their home.

"Unusual" he thought. There must be something special tonight, maybe. Oh no, did I forget her birthday, or is it our anniversary? To his dismay, no usual hugs or kisses, no "how was your day," only a waving of her hands and arms and finger pointing in my direction.

I was at work. I had been sent into that neighborhood by my boss to final grade two homes. That means you spread the top soil and prepare the soil for seed which would produce green lawns.

One thing I had learned over the years that I had worked on construction was to always take a few minutes to walk the property prior to moving any ground, taking time to check and see if anything may have been left behind or might possibly be concealed by the high grass and weeds on the property.

Upon checking the property where I was to work, I did find a TV line partially buried with other sections above the ground. I immediately used the two-way radio to contact my boss, who in turn phoned the building contractor. In a few minutes the building contractor was on site. I was informed to cut the exposed line as this was not a service to the home. Possibly the TV line installer had left the unused line lay, and when the ditch was backfilled, this part remained uncovered. All this took place prior to my moving any ground that morning.

Oh, by the way I did forget to mention that this home was on the lot next to the one where this woman was having a real challenge. This may have had something to do with her being extremely upset.

After completing the final grade of that home and cutting the cable numerous times, I then moved across the street, where the second home was located. This is where I was, when I saw everything that was happening between the man and his wife. In fact, I had a front row seat. It was like looking at a large screen television in living color. I was witnessing all that was happening, but I could not hear what was being said.

Just what was this woman complaining about to her husband? Could she be upset with the noise created by the dozer I was operating? I knew, according to township regulations, they had a noise ordinance, which was in effect from eight o'clock in the evening to seven o'clock in the morning, but I did not start running the machine until approximately seven-thirty in the morning. No way was I at fault, I thought. The thought entered my mind: she possibly is upset and is complaining to her husband about the rough condition of their lawn and how good these two lots were looking.

I did not know, and truthfully I did not really care about this woman. If she had a problem, or the reason she was acting in this manner, was no concern of mine. However, her actions had caught my attention.

It was only a few minutes after his arrival home, before he was headed in my direction. This man stood about five-feet eight- inches tall. His arms and shoulders were ones that definitely indicated he had spent many hours developing them in a gym. He looked like a gorilla on a path of destruction as he headed my way!

Quick as a flash, without any invitation on my part, he jumped up onto the dozer and was only inches from me. He was in a sate of anger as he proceeded to air his complaint to me. Little did I realize that he had a very limited vocabulary, not consisting of more than four or five words, none of which I will write about.

Still unaware of what had angered this man, I remained calm. Perhaps it was my calmness that drove him to make his next move. Standing only inches from me, he reared back, and his fist, which was attached to his muscular arm, was headed full-force in the direction of my face and jaw.

There was no time for plea bargaining. He was past the point of no return. He was about to do an extreme make-over on me.

At that moment in time, all I could do was cry out the name of Jesus. Nothing more, nothing less. Only the name, "Jesus!" Instantly, as the name "Jesus" was spoken, this man froze. His fist ended up only inches from the point of impact, which was my jaw.

That man stood there frozen in place. Finally, he was able to speak and said, "What did you say? I don't understand. I should have busted your jaw or nose, but it was as though I hit a concrete wall."

The power of the name of Jesus had just saved me.

What had happened to anger this woman was the fact that I had cut the TV line to their home. Somehow the property lines had been changed, and their TV line was now located on someone else's property. Poor woman, I thought, she will have to wait for another day to find out what happened on "Days of Our Lives."

This man finally gained his composure and apologized for the language he had just used. His final question to me was, "That name, 'Jesus,' does it always contain enough power to stop a man out-of-control?"

I thought about David and how he informed Goliath, "You come with all your armor, but I come to you in the name of the Lord."

"In the day when I cried out, You answered me..."
(Psalm 138:3a)

As I stood (actually I was sitting) in the shadow of the giant I was facing, my confidence was not in someone else's armor, but in the name of Jesus. Thank God, He was not on vacation or taking a nap. The split second I cried out, He heard and answered me.

Questions Only You Can Answer

Chapter 13 "On the Road to Facing the Giants in Life"

As you travel the "On the road to ... ," how many Goliaths have you encountered so far?

Has their physical structure left you feeling like a mouse or a man?

How convincing have their words been, leaving you in a state of defeat?

Is it possible there has been a time or two when you have acted like Goliath, and because of what you said, you brought fear into someone's life?

Have you ever found yourself in a position where the only thing you could say was the name, "Jesus"?

Presently, what is your level of faith?

Are you one hundred percent sure if this very minute you cried out, that God would recognize your voice and rescue you from an adversary you were facing?

Chapter 14

On the Road to Receiving God's Details

U p to this point in my life I had gone through many valleys and climbed many mountains. I had made some wise decisions and others which I regretted. I knew the promise I had made to the Lord the day I lay on that hospital litter: "Lord, if You deliver me from this addiction, I will serve you the rest of my life." He upheld His part, and I wanted my word to be as good as I had spoken.

Still having the desire to serve the Lord, I prayed and asked God, "Show me Your plan for my life. Make it so clear I have no doubt as to where I should go or what I should do." In doing so my prayer was about to be answered.

"Now Jericho was securely shut up because of the children of Israel; none went out, and none came in. And the Lord said to Joshua: 'See! I have given Jericho into your hand, its king, and the mighty men of valor. You shall march around the city, all you men of war; you shall go all around the city once. This you shall do six days. And seven priests shall bear seven trumpets of rams' horns before the

ark. But the seventh day you shall march around the city seven times, and the priests shall blow the trumpets. It shall come to pass, when they make a long blast with the ram's horn, and when you hear the sound of the trumpet, then all the people shall shout with a great shout; then the wall of the city will fall down flat. And the people shall go up every man straight before him.'" (Joshua 6:1-5)

God was very specific in His instructions to Joshua. Remember, I had prayed and asked God to reveal His plan for my life. God knew the proper time, and now He was about to reveal it to me.

After going to India and then Honduras on two outreaches, now God was saying, "It's time to go to a new land that I am going to reveal to you."

It was when I was attending a service at a prominent church in Lancaster, Pennsylvania, that I heard the pastor say they were looking for men to go to Mexico. Once again I had heard, and it was time to become a doer and not a hearer only. I, along with my son Duane, signed up and became part of this outreach.

It was on this trip that my ears would be opened as God would reveal *part* of His plan for my life. I say *part* as it has been my experience over the many years of walking with the Lord, that He would only reveal to me what I was capable of handling at that specific time.

One day as we were traveling in a pick-up truck to a remote village, high up in the mountains of central Mexico, I asked the driver to stop. I got out and moved to the back of the truck. It was from here I would be able to get a better view of the surroundings and a much better recording advantage. This was an area of utmost beauty, with mountains on both sides, as well as rocks, cacti, and gullies which we had to cross. There were no roads, no markers, only a path made by ox-drawn carts. This is what we followed the many miles leading to the place where we were headed.

As I stood on the rear of this truck videotaping, something happened. It was extremely windy. I could feel the wind as it blew against my body. I heard its sound, and then without warning, it was though I had gone deaf. Standing there, deaf to the sound of the wind and my surroundings, I heard the Lord speak to me as He said, "In response to your prayers, I have brought you to this place."

I have always been the type of person who, when asking for something of great importance, does not only want to hear the response, but I want to be shown as well. You need to understand, I had asked God to show me the place where He wanted me to "go and preach". I wanted to be one hundred percent positive, no doubting or guessing, and this was His way of letting me know this was it.

"Lord, how can this be? There is no one here, not even one house?" Silence began to overwhelm me as we continued on our journey. Within a few miles as we were descending down a mountainside, I noticed something off in the distance. It was a village consisting of about six homes and the walls of what was to be a church building.

Upon arrival at that village, we were greeted by a woman and her children, and immediately the woman came up to me and gave me a kiss on my cheek. This was God's way of confirming to me what He had spoken to me a few minutes earlier as I was riding in the back of the truck.

"Lord, is this for real? Surely You don't want me to spend the rest of my days in a place like this, do You? Lord, could we discuss this at a later time when my head is clear, as it has been a long journey, and I am tired and hungry?"

That day we spent as much time as we could at that ranch.. We knew that we had to leave at least two hours prior to sunset. We were conscious of the fact that it would be impossible to find our way back in the dark of night. All this was part of God's plan for my life. He did what He deemed necessary to get my attention, even if it was to have me travel to some desolate place high in the mountains of Mexico.

Upon returning back to the United States a few days later, still not being sure of what all this meant, I began to seriously ask God for more details.

Now came a challenge. What if God is going to send us to Mexico on assignment? We were growing and experiencing ministry full force. The security of receiving a paycheck weekly was comforting, but we loved ministering to the people. The challenge was giving it all up, stepping out in faith, believing God would supply our every need. The hardest decision we would have to make was to walk away from that sense of security.

Our pastor and his wife were great. They had treated us well. They invested much leadership training into our lives, and we remain grateful for all their influence in our lives.

God was about to unveil more of His plan. It was revealed to me that it was not just that village He would have me return to, but that we were being sent on assignment to Mexico.

"Why me, Lord?" I asked, since I did not speak the language or truly understand the culture.

"You are to go as you have committed to and as I have commissioned you to do. I will supply for you what you need and when you need it."

From that point in time, God would have many assignments that He would send us on. Not only would it involve going into Mexico numerous times, but also expanding our area of influence into the Philippines, Jamaica, and the United States, beside our having been to India and Honduras, and more recently to Ecuador.

The time came when we had to leave our home and family and move into Mexico. Receiving God's details was exciting and rewarding, although sometimes extremely painful. Being doers of His Word became our lifestyle. As we continued to be led by the Holy Spirit, we preached the gospel and witnessed many people being saved, baptized, and filled with the Holy Spirit. Receiving God's details made us aware that there was a need for developing leaders.

"And He Himself gave some to be apostles, some prophets, some evangelists, and some pastors and teachers, for the equipping pf the saints for the work of ministry, for the edifying of the body of Christ." (Ephesians 4:11-12)

Seeing or hearing of a need is only step one. This must be followed by step two, and that is to be a doer.

We developed, with the help of God, a leadership training plan, "Training Leaders of the Nations to Make a Difference." We traveled about teaching in many areas, helping prepare the saints for the work of ministry.

The sacrifices Nancy and I have had to make are minimal to the results we have seen as we have had opportunity after opportunity to sow seeds, His Word, into the lives of countless numbers of people.

My prayer for all who have taken the time to read this book to this point, is that you who have ears to hear, will hear. As you hear from Him, which is step one, why not continue on and do step two: walk out His plan for your life? Be a doer of the Word of God.

Questions Only You Can Answer

Chapter 14 "On the Road to Receiving God's Details"

Are you a person who needs details in everything you do?

Do you focus on the natural things instead of the supernatural?

When if ever, have you received specific instruction from God, pertaining to a mission or ministry He had for your life?

Do you believe in journaling, writing down what God reveals to you?

Do you have a hard time witnessing to others?

Do you have a hard time witnessing to men and women who have been called into a place of leadership?

Are you a person who has a tendency to procrastinate?

Are you the type person who is led by the Spirit in making all major decisions in your lie?

Chapter 15

On the Road to Walking Out His Plan

"Then He taught them many things by parables, and said unto them in His teaching: 'Listen! Behold, a sower went out to sow. And it happened as he sowed, that some seed fell by the wayside; and the birds of the air came and devoured it. Some fell on stony ground, where it did not have much earth; and immediately it sprang up because it had no depth of earth. But when the sun was up it was scorched, and because it had no root it withered away. And some seed fell among the thorns; and the thorns grew up and choked it, and it yielded no crop. But other seed fell on good ground and yielded a crop that sprang up, increased and produced: some thirtyfold, some sixty, and some a hundred.' And He said to them, 'He who has ears to hear, let him hear!'"
(Mark 4:2-9)

After reading these verses of scripture, I had to stop and do a self-examination. I had heard the Word, and the Word being the seed, and the soil being me, what was I yielding? Which one of these was the type soil I was? Had the seed fallen by the wayside, because I had been so preoccupied? How deep was my level of faith, and how deep did my roots go? What if anything was stealing the life out of me?

What was my yield ratio? Was there a thirtyfold, sixty, or a hundred yield or none at all? These were the questions I asked myself. What was God's plan for my life? He did say in **Mark 4:9, "He has ears to hear, let him hear,"** did He not?

I had ears, and yes, I had heard:

"And He said to them, 'Go into all the world and preach the gospel to every creature. He who believes and is baptized will be saved; but he who does not will be condemned. And these signs will follow those who believe: In My name they will cast our demons; they will speak with new tongues; they will take up serpents; and if they drink anything deadly, it will by no means hurt them; they will lay hands on the sick, and they will recover.'" (Mark 16:15-18)

Now the rest was up to me. I had heard and now another process had begun to develop.

"But be doers of the word, and not hearers only, deceiving yourselves." (James 1:22)

The word, **"Go into all the world and preach the gospel to every creature", (Mark 16:15)** was the seed, and now I was the soil which had to respond, or else I was only deceiving myself.

One evening I had gone to bed and was sound asleep when I heard the voice of God. These were His instructions and details as to what I was to do:

"You are to start a ministry called 'Operation A-Vision'. You are to collect 80 thousand pounds of clothing and ship them to Mexico. You are to take a team of people to Mexico the third week of March. You are to contact area pastors and tell them about the vision, and you are never to ask for financial aid."

I actually heard God speak these details to me. As He did, I lay there in my bed unable to move. Was this for real? Did God mean me or was this for someone else? Maybe it was for my wife! As I lay there, I heard the clock strike midnight. I knew my hearing was okay, so could it be that I really did hear from God?

Within moments I heard the exact details again. This time I got out of bed and headed to our office, where I began to record what He had revealed to me. Within minutes the details were revealed the third time. There was no guessing or doubting. I had written what I had heard from Him. Although some may doubt or question what I had heard, no one, not even Satan, was ever going to steal these details from me. I had been taught, if you hear something, and you wish to retain it forever, write it down, just as the men inspired by God did in recording the Word (the Bible). Past experiences had taught me that unless I record something the minute I hear it, a time will come when a voice will be speaking directly into my ears telling me, "This is not what you heard."

I knew that I knew I had received God's details for my life and the ministry He had for us.

Early that morning, I got up as I had a commitment to fulfill. I had committed to drive the pastor my wife worked for, to the airport. The entire way to the airport and all the way back home, my mind was trying to comprehend the instructions the Lord had just given to me.

When I arrived home, my wife was waiting very intensely to talk to me. She had found the notes I had written with all the instructions and was a bit irritated. She also said that when she realized that I had gotten out of bed at midnight, her first thought was that I was not being true to the diet we had just started that day, that I was sneaking food into the office to eat. She said she did get out of bed and peek into the office to see if I was eating anything, but what she saw was that I was writing something.

When I asked her if she believed the Lord had spoken to me, she had a look on her face that said, "Oh brother!" Oddly enough, as she had been sitting in her favorite recliner that morning, lying on a table next to her, was a small ministry book which she picked up. She said, "I believe you." Although I doubted what you had written about what the Lord had revealed to you, as I picked up that book, it opened to page twenty-three. And there were the words *'A-Vision'* in very large print." She said, "Look." As she opened the book to show me the print, it was now the same size print as the rest of the book.

"Then the Lord, answered me and said: 'Write the vision and make it plain on tablets, that he may run who reads it. For the vision is yet for an appointed time; but at the end it will speak, and it will not lie. Though it tarries, wait for it; because it will surely come, it will not tarry.'"
(Habakkuk 2:2-3)

God had inspired me to write the vision. It was in black and white, and all we had to do was "not be a parked car." We needed to put ourselves into motion, and then He would be able to steer us in the direction He would have us go.

My wife had questions: How was this all going to happen? What would we have to do to get this vision into operation? And how does God expect us to do all He was requiring of us without asking for financial assistance?

Unable to answer her questions, as I did not know the answers, the only thing I could assure her of was, if God had said it, then it would happen!

What had been revealed to me earlier that day left me in a state of dependency. I was not a person to stand before men of God and openly share from my heart. That was outside of my comfort zone.

"Jesus said to him, 'If you can believe, all things are possible to him who believes.'" (Mark 9:23)

I not only believed that I had heard from God, I knew it. These things would happen as God had spoken. How, when, or why I did not know. All I was certain of was that according to what I had heard, God was birthing a new ministry called "Operation A-Vision", and Nancy and I were going to be an intricate part of this ministry.

Procrastination had no place in my mind, and I knew we had to act, not as a parked vehicle, but as willing vessels.

"In whom we have boldness and access with confidence through faith in Him." (Ephesians 3:12)

"And with great power the apostles gave witness to the resurrection of the Lord Jesus. And great grace was upon them all." (Acts 4:33)

I started making phone calls to area pastors, and by evening I had appointments with seven, who were willing to listen to the vision God had given to me. I also made a phone call to the missionary we were working with at that time in Mexico. After checking his schedule of upcoming groups, he informed me that the only week he had open was the third week of March. I immediately informed him that I wanted to reserve that week for a group that would be accompanying us. This I spoke in faith as no one had even mentioned that they had a desire to join us on a trip into Mexico. How would people ever find out what we were doing?

Things were progressing so fast, it reminded me of the time we were asked to go to India. Surely this was God, for no man could do what was happening. Eighty thousand pounds of clothing (forty tons) is a lot of clothing, so we asked the Lord, "Where are we going to get all this clothing?"

Three days after receiving God's detailed instructions, we attended a service at a well-known church in Allentown, Pennsylvania. After sharing the vision with the pastor, he informed us that they had bags of clothing that they wanted to donate to missions. We knew God had started the work.

The Vision Goes Public

I had given a written copy of the vision God had given me to a local newspaper. The newspaper printed it word for word, even printing the name "God" several times.

As time progressed, we received many donations of used clothing, all of which had to be sorted prior to shipping. Our two car garage was converted into a sorting area, where we had nothing more than two old desks to work on and some makeshift shelving. Clothing, shoes and household items came in by the bagful, as we had gone public with the vision. After the clothing was checked and found suitable for shipping, everything needed to be boxed, and then stored until we had a tractor-trailer load.

With all these things arriving daily, there arose some challenges. First, we needed boxes in which to store the merchandise. My wife had the answer. She would take our grandchildren to the local supermarkets and stores, and place them into the dumpsters, and they would retrieve any boxes which had been discarded.

Second, because we had very limited space in our garage, we needed storage space. There were times we would have ten to fifteen people working in our garage, and there was no place to stack the filled boxes. God supernaturally laid it on people's hearts to let us use spaces they had in basements, barns, and pole buildings. We utilized everything given to us.

The time came when we tried to calculate if we had enough boxes to fill a tractor-trailer. We assumed we did. But now the question came as to how would we get those boxes from Pennsylvania to Texas. We had no money, as everything we were doing was being done by volunteers, and God had said, " You are never to ask for financial aid." The thought came that maybe God had forgotten to give me those details, or possibly He had overlooked the fact that we would have to transport these boxes.

God had the answer, so we prayed and asked Him. He supernaturally had made the arrangements. All we had to do was listen, and when He said, "Go to the phone, and call Four Seasons Trucking from Lancaster, Pennsylvania," the answer would be revealed. The exact time came for us to contact this trucking company. They agreed to come to our home and pick up this load of merchandise and transport it to Texas without a charge. Praise the Lord, we were on the way to fulfilling the 80 thousand pounds that the Lord had said we should ship.

Saturday morning came, the day we had made arrangements to load the trailer. Many men, women, and children had come out to assist in the loading process. We had a construction company, who graciously lent us a cube van, which we used to go to all the storage areas, where we had boxes stored, and to haul them to our home.

The heavy rains didn't stop us from getting the job done. In less than three hours, we had the entire trailer loaded. Upon getting the trailer weighed, we were informed that the weight was 18 thousand pounds. That was a good start to reaching our goal of 80 thousand pounds.

More and more items came in. We had many volunteers including Girl Scouts and Boy Scouts, who would come out and spend hours assisting us. It was a lot of fun and also a great time of fellowship. Everyday when Nancy came home from her job at the church, she would prepare homemade goodies for that night. Everyone who came enjoyed them, while assisting in the sorting and boxing.

Bags full of clothing filled pick-up trucks. No longer were our grandchildren able to keep up with the demand for boxes. Praise the Lord, a local box company gave us pallets of new, unused boxes. We also had someone who donated a pole barn for us to use to store more of the filled boxes.

One day I received a phone call from a man who wanted to give us 6 thousand pairs of shoes. These shoes had been salvaged from a flooded warehouse. They were not sized or sorted, but had been thrown at random into storage containers. Most were salvageable, but needed cleaning and to be matched and sized.

The storage areas were once again filled to the brim, and it was time for another shipment. No problem, we thought. We will just call Four Seasons and tell them we have another load ready to be taken to Texas. Contact was made and much to our surprise, we were informed that they would not be able to help us at that time.

God had the answer, so why not pray and ask Him? As we prayed, once again He supernaturally had made the arrangements. This was happening at a time when I was employed as an associate pastor at a local church. One day someone had handed me a slip of paper with the name of a trucking company written on it. I had forgotten about this note, but when we needed someone to take this next load, I remembered. I gave the note to my wife. She phoned Ethan Good Trucking. After explaining the vision to Mr. Good, he responded that his company would take a load to Texas without a charge to the ministry. He agreed to have a tractor-trailer at our home on the Saturday we had designated.

Loading day came, and this time, not only did we have sufficient help to load the trailer, we had a big surprise. A local television station had sent a reporter, and he recorded the process of loading the trailer. It was broadcast that evening on the local news. During our acts of obedience, we were also interviewed on several Christian TV talk shows.

Time marched on, and we now had what we believed to be the third load. All we needed to do was to make a phone call, and it would be on the way. Nancy contacted the first trucking company, to which they respond with a "no", and the second said "no" as well.

There was nowhere to turn except to God, for only He had the answer. Why not pray and ask Him? Pray we did, and once again, He supernaturally had made the arrangements. All we had to do was listen, and when He said to go to the phone and call Transport for Christ from Lancaster, Pennsylvania, the answer would be revealed. The time came when Nancy felt prompted to make the call.

It seemed that the person to whom Nancy had spoken to, had just transferred from Missouri to Pennsylvania. Transport for Christ is a mobile chapel ministry of which this man was a member and although he knew of no trucking company in that immediate area that could possibly help us, he did know of a company from Missouri.

A company from Missouri! How crazy to think they would come to Pennsylvania and take a load to Texas for us!

The time had come, the exact minute when Nancy was prompted to make the next call. She had been informed that she should ask to speak to a man named Moose, who was the owner of the trucking company. When the phone call was answered, Nancy heard the name of the company. It is Genesis Trucking. After sharing the vision with the secretary, she informed Nancy that she was going to transfer her to the owner of the company. "Hello. This is Moose. How can I help you?"

When Nancy heard that she was talking to Moose, the person she was told to ask for, she said, "You're just the person I need to talk to." She explained the vision to him and that we needed to transport boxes of clothing from Pennsylvania to Texas for the Mexican people, and that it had to be done without charge to the ministry.

God's timing is extremely important. We must move when He says move and wait when He says wait. It appeared that only fifteen minutes prior to my wife's making contact with this company that the dispatcher had approached Moose. It was at this time he had informed him of a new account they had just acquired. It was in Allentown, Pennsylvania, which was approximately ten miles from where our ministry was located. Moose told us that we had found our trucking company. Genesis Trucking transported six loads for us. Only God could arrange for a trucking company from Missouri to come to Pennsylvania to meet the need.

We had met the vision of 80 thousand pounds with the first three loads that were shipped and exceeded it abundantly. In the process of collecting, sorting, boxing, and shipping this clothing, several people accepted Jesus into their lives through our witnessing to them. Three of these were the truck drivers. In just seven months we had collected and shipped the 80 thousand pounds. We exceeded it by continuing to collect items.

During this time many had heard about the vision. We had a group of people who had committed to accompany us on a trip into Mexico. It was going to happen the third week of March, just as God had said. This group of men and women were excited to see what God was about to do.

One man had read about the vision in the newspaper and had volunteered to go. He had just gone through a dramatic time in his life. His wife had committed suicide, and he needed answers to many questions he had. God had a divine plan for him. He prayed and asked Jesus into his life, while in our van, as we were traveling seventy miles per hour down a highway in Mexico.

The group accomplished much as we worked on a church, located way up in the mountains in Mexico. We were able to put a roof over their newly constructed building. Clothing was given away, and people were touched as the team members gave away the shoes they were wearing, having to return to our motel barefooted. What a blessing it was for everyone. God ministered to the hearts of all the team members and used them as a mighty witness for Him. We pray that they will always remember what happened on that trip and will never be the same again.

Questions Only You Can Answer

Chapter 15 "On the Road to Walking Out His Plan"

Seeing yourself as soil and the seed being sown as the Word, what type soil do you see yourself as being?
Soil by the wayside
Shallow with depth
Scorched, dry, and dusty
Thorn-infested
Good, productive with a high percentage of yield

Is there any positive yield coming from your soil?

If so what is your percentage of yield, 30 – 60 – 100?

Are your ears open to the voice of the Living Word?

How have you responded to the command, "Go ...
to your family?"
to your neighborhood?"
to your friends?"
into all the world?"

If you have gone as commanded, have you witnessed salvations, people being baptized with water, and then being filled with the Holy Spirit?

Do you see yourself as a doer or only as a hearer of His word?

If you are a doer, what signs have you seen being done in the name of Jesus?

When was the last time you have shared your testimony with an unsaved person?

On a scale of one to ten, ten being the highest, where do you see yourself as being obedient to walking out His plan for your life?

If your response to the last question is not near a ten, then what would you say is keeping you from a potential ten?

Now that you have examined yourself, and you have admitted your shortcomings, why not pray and ask God to remove all these hindrances from your life?

Chapter 16

On the Road to a Hard Lesson to Learn

"Now it came to pass after these things that God tested Abraham, and said to him, 'Abraham!' And he said, 'Here I am.'

"Then He said, 'Take now your son, your only son Isaac, whom you love, and go to the land of Moriah, and offer him there as a burnt offering on one of the mountains of which I shall tell you.'

"So Abraham rose early in the morning and saddled his donkey, and took two of his young men with him, and Isaac his son; and he split the wood for the burnt offering, and arose and went to the place of which God had told him.
"Then on the third day Abraham lifted his eyes and saw the place afar off.

"And Abraham said to his young men, 'Stay here with the donkey; the lad and I will go yonder and worship, and we will come back to you.'

"So Abraham took the wood of the burnt offering and laid it on Isaac his son; and he took the fire in his hand, and a knife, and the two of them went together.

"But Isaac spoke to Abraham his father and said, 'My father!' And he said, 'Here I am, my son.' Then he said, 'Look the fire and the wood, but where is the lamb for a burnt offering?'

"And Abraham said, 'My son, God will provide for Himself the lamb for a burnt offering.' So the two of them went together.

"Then they came to the place of which God had told him. And Abraham built an altar there and placed the wood in order; and he bound Isaac his son and laid him on the altar, upon the wood.

"And Abraham stretched out his hand and took the knife to slay his son. But the Angel of the Lord called to him from heaven and said, 'Abraham, Abraham!' So he said, 'Here I am.'

"And He said, 'Do not lay your hand on the lad, or do anything to him; for now I know that you fear God, since you have not withheld you son, your only son, from Me.'" (Genesis 22:1-12)

Abraham feared God. He feared Him to a point that he was willing to sacrifice his only son, Isaac, if that was what God wanted from him. God's instructions were very explicit. He had instructed Abraham what he was to take with him and what he was to do.

I am sure Abraham may have asked himself this question, "Why would God ask me to sacrifice my only son? He knows how much I love him." As far out as it may have seemed to Abraham, he was going to be obedient to God even if it cost him his son's life.

I mentioned in the previous chapter that God had instructed us to collect 80 thousand pounds of clothing and ship them to Texas for less fortunate people of Mexico. This was accomplished with the first three loads that we had shipped.

As we continued collecting, sorting, boxing and then shipping beyond the 80 thousand pounds, it wasn't long before things began to take a turn. After a few more loads, it seem everything we tried to do became more and more difficult. Volunteers were becoming weary and finding less time to give to the vision. One man, whose truck was being used quite frequently to pick up clothing, sustained a broken windshield, while picking up some clothing. He had come seeking financial compensation from the ministry, finances which we did not have.

At this time, although a few monetary donations had come into the ministry, the majority of this was used to buy tape to seal the boxes for shipment. People also had asked us to no longer store boxes in some of their storage areas as they had other needs for these rooms or buildings. The supply of used clothing kept coming in, but something was not right.

One evening a friend named Minnie visited our home. We spent time talking about the ministry. She then made this comment, "The reason things have become difficult is because you are out the will of God."

How could this be? There was a need, and it was being fulfilled through our ministry. How could this not be the will of God? She then proceeded to ask me about the original vision God had given me concerning the 80 thousand pounds.

I had to admit He did say 80 thousand pounds. He did not say, "You are to continue collecting and shipping clothing, until I tell you to stop."

Because of our eagerness to serve Him in what we were doing, we missed one very important fact: only do as God had instructed. No more. No less. Immediately we disbanded all collecting and shipping of clothing. Oh, how easy it was to get sidetracked and get off course.

It was in that time that I realized how easy it would have been for Abraham to get sidetracked. Had he gotten off course or out of God's timing, it could have cost him his son's life.

"My brethren, count it all joy when you fall into various trials, knowing that the testing of your faith produces patience. But let patience have its perfect work, that you may be perfect and complete, lacking nothing. If any of you lacks wisdom, let him ask of God, who gives to all liberally and without reproach, and it will be given to him." (James 1:2-4)

How many more times will I have to go through the times of testing and only do as I'm told? I know that as long as I have breath left in me, I will go through times of testing. "Lord, I admit, it is the patience to endure that I ask of You, and as I ask, You will liberally give without reproach."

"Blessed is the man who endures temptation; for when he has been approved, he will receive the crown of life which the Lord has promised to those who love Him." (James 1:12)

"Lord, I pray for wisdom, in all things I do, and I will do them with Your blessing."

Questions Only You Can Answer

Chapter 16 "On the Road to a Hard Lesson to Learn"

Do you reverently fear of the Lord?

Have you ever been asked by the Lord to make an unusual sacrifice, one you did not comprehend?

Have you ever heard your name being called by the Lord, and did you respond with "Here I am"?

Do you believe parameters are good and that we must remain within the boundaries God has set for each of us?

Are you the type of person who is easily sidetracked, or do you stick to the course set before you?

Can you name a time when you know you went beyond what God had instructed you to do?

Do you consider it a "joyful" time when God is purging you and when you are going through a time of testing?

Chapter 17

On the Road to Staying Connected

In this book I have mentioned the many roads we have traveled on in our life's journey. All roads will lead you somewhere, even if some will have detours or lead you to a dead end.

You may encounter many blind curves, dangerous intersections, huge mountains, and deep valleys along the way, and you will be tested as you travel through all kinds of weather conditions. Sun-beaten pathways, rain-soaked roads, snow and ice-covered lanes of travel will all present challenges along the way. You must say connected so as not to lose direction and veer off course.

"'I am the true vine, and My Father is the vine-dresser. Every branch in Me that does not bear fruit, He takes away; and every branch that bears fruit He prunes, that it may bear more fruit. You are already clean because of the word which I have spoken to you. Abide in Me, and I in you. As the branch cannot bear fruit of itself, unless it abides in the vine, neither can you, unless you abide in Me. I am the vine, you are the branches. He who

abides in Me, and I in him, bears much fruit; for without Me you can do nothing. If anyone does not abide in Me, he is cast out as a branch and is withered; and they gather them and throw them into the fire, and they are burned. If you abide in Me, and My words abide in you, you will ask what you desire, and it shall be done for you. By this My Father is glorified, that you bear much fruit; so you will be My disciples." (John 15:1-8)

Scriptures are very clear that we need to remain connected. There are many life applications which one can relate to about remaining connected. One such experience which I want to describe to you is parasailing.

In order to go parasailing one must have access to a device made up of metal, plastic, and fabric. Then when it is properly assembled and pulled by the necessary towing device in water, it will lift a person or persons up off the water and suspend him or her in the air as long as the towline remains taut and certain air pressure is maintained.

I have observed people actually being harnessed into such a device and then pulled by a boat, rising above the waters. The towline was the only thing that connected the people in the sailing device to the boat. A break in the towline could create a dangerous situation, leaving those airborne to be at the mercy of the winds. A boat running out of fuel, causing the speed to decrease, would result in the sailing device not remaining airborne. Going with the air currents, and not against them, would create a problem. The people in the flying device are at the mercy of the person operating the boat. He has control of their situation as long as the towline, their lifeline, remains connected and taut. If their towline, their lifeline was severed, they would be headed on the road to disaster.

As I observed these people, joyfully paras
15:1-8 took on a new meaning in my life. A new reve___
of the Word had just appeared before my very eyes. As long
as I stay connected with the Lord, I am on the road to bearing
fruit. Break the connection, sever myself from the True Vine,
and I am on the road to disaster.

"My people are destroyed for lack of knowledge..." (Hosea 4:6a)

We need to pursue and value godly knowledge and
wisdom, with the understanding that what we do not know
can hurt us. I have heard people say time and time again,
"What I don't know won't hurt me." We can go on trying
to make excuses for the things of life we have intentionally
done, but God's word clearly states that because of the lack
of knowledge, His people are destroyed.

How foolish I think one would be to just decide to let go
of the towline when they were parasailing. That is, unless
they had not received advice or counsel from someone who
had knowledge of the importance of not severing or drop-
ping the towline. Would anyone be so foolish to not have
an understanding and some knowledge of the importance of
staying connected?

How does one bear fruit? I look outside my home, and
I see trees and vines all bearing fruit. It is then that I realize
that as long as they are connected and receive nourishment
from the main source, they have the capabilities of producing
more fruit.

However the scripture does not end there.

"I anyone does not abide in Me, he is cast out as a branch and is withered: and they gather them and throw them into the fire, and they are burned." (John 15:6)

My thoughts once again go back to the verse of scripture in **Hosea 4:6**, where the Lord says, **"My people are destroyed for the lack of knowledge."**

Why, I cry out, Lord, why are so many perishing? His response was simply this, "Because of the lack of knowledge."

"Hear, my son, and receive my sayings, and the years of your life will be many. I have taught you in the way of wisdom: I have led you in the right paths. When you walk, your steps will not be hindered, and when you run, you will not stumble. Take firm hold of instruction, do not let go; keep her, for she is your life." (Proverbs 4:10-13)

"Lord, help me through those times when my hands become tired, and I am about to lose my grip. Lord, I thank You that as You lead me on the road to ... , that my steps will not be hindered."

"Then Jesus went about all the cities and villages, teaching in their synagogues, preaching the gospel of the kingdom, and healing every sickness and every disease among the people. But when He saw the multitudes, He was moved with compassion for them, because they were weary and scattered, like sheep having no shepherd. Then He said to His disciples, 'The harvest truly is plentiful, but the laborers are few.'" (Matthew 9:35-37)

These are the words I heard from the Lord, followed by, "Can I count on you? Are you connected?"

With this I had a flashback in time. I heard the words of my earthly father that he told me as a child, "Work hard; always give and do your best; do unto others as you would

expect them to do to you; don't ever be late fo
meeting; nothing in life is free; do as you said y
your word must be like a legal document; and d̲.. ....
I'll find out the truth."

"Yes! Yes! Lord, You can count on me. I want to do my
part. I am not disconnecting or letting go of my lifeline.
Lord, what must be done to decrease the number of people
who will perish because of their lack of knowledge?"

**"For 'whoever calls on the name of the Lord
shall be saved.' How then shall they call on Him
in whom they have not believed? And how shall
they believe in Him of whom they have not heard?
And how shall they hear without a preacher? And
how shall they preach unless they are sent? As it is
written: 'How beautiful are the feet of those who
preach the gospel of peace, who bring glad tidings
of good things!'" (Romans 10:13-15)**

"This," says the Lord, "is your assignment. This is how
there will be a decline in the number of people who perish
for lack of knowledge."

**"How God anointed Jesus of Nazareth with the
Holy Spirit and with power, who went about doing
good and healing all who were oppressed by the
devil, for God was with Him." (Acts 10:38)**

"Not only are you to go and preach with a higher degree
of calling and anointing, I am also releasing a new anointing
upon your life. One, the anointing for healing is about to be
manifested in your life with signs and wonders following.
My supernatural healing power not only will be evident in
My Word, but it will also be witnessed by many as you do

according to My Word, lay hands on the sick, and they will recover."

I, says the Lord, challenge you to take a close look at your hands. Are they any different than those of Paul? **"Now God worked unusual miracles by the hands of Paul."** (**Acts 19:11**) God can and will work miracles through your hands, if you let Him.

As the Lord continues on, He says: "I am about to release a new seer anointing upon your life."

> **"Then Jesus answered and said to them: 'Most assuredly, I say to you, the Son can do nothing of Himself, but what He sees the Father do; for whatever He does, the Son also does in like manner. For the Father loves the Son, and shows Him all things that He Himself does; and He will show Him greater works than these. that you may marvel.'" (John 5:19-20)**

"Because of your relationship with My Son Jesus, and the power of the Holy Spirit living inside you, I," says the Lord, "will show you things to come, although you will not always know when or where they will happen, but they will in My time. Look all around you. The fields are white for harvest! Tarry not!"

> **"For you have need of endurance, so that after you have done the will of God, you may receive the promise: 'For yet a little while, and He who is coming will come and will not tarry. Now the just shall live by faith; but if anyone draws back, My soul has no pleasure in him.'"**
> **(Hebrews 10:36-38)**

Questions Only You Can Answer

Chapter 17 "On the Road to Staying Connected

Do you believe that not everyone is required to stand behind a pulpit, as in a church, to declare the Word of the Lord?

Since a person's pulpit is the place where they have been ordained to minister the Word, such as in their home, their place of employment, the local neighborhood corner, to children, to youth, to seniors in a nursing home, in hospitals, etc., where is your pulpit?

How consistent are you in your times and places of ministry?

Are you in need of more endurance to finish the course set before you?

Chapter 18

On the Road to a New Season

"To everything there is a season, a time for every purpose under heaven: a time to be born, and a time to die; a time to plant, and a time to pluck what is planted; a time to kill, and a time to heal; a time to break down, and a time to build up; a time to weep, and a time to laugh; a time to mourn, and a time to dance; a time to cast away stones, and a time to gather stones; a time to embrace, and a time to refrain from embracing; a time to gain, and a time to lose; a time to keep, and a time to throw away; a time to tear, and a time to sew; a time to keep silence, and a time to speak; a time to love, and a time to hate; a time of war, and a time of peace." (Ecclesiastes 3:1-8)

Having traveled thousands of miles on many roads, through all types of obstacles and conditions, I was to embark on a new season of my life. I had experienced God's supernatural ability and power to provide for whatever challenges I was facing and those of others I met along the journey.

God had given us, Nancy and me, many opportunities to minister His word with signs and wonders following. We had experienced His provision as both of us had given up our jobs and were now living totally dependent on Him for all our needs.

We had, with the help and support of friends and churches, purchased land and built two large churches in Matehuala, Mexico. We also had purchased property and built a home in Mexico for a very needy woman and her three children, who, when we first met, were living in a structure made out of nothing more than scrap tin, cardboard, and plastic. We had ministered to men, women, youth, and children by the thousands. Many people made decisions to turn from their earthly ways and have Jesus fill the void in their lives and give them the assurance of eternal life with Him.

Not ever having attended a Bible School and not having credentials according to the world's standards, we faced many challenges. However, both of us had received Certificates of Ordination. Times came when pastors, men and woman, would come up to us and say, "What year did you say you graduated from so-and-so Bible Training Center?" When they heard our response, "We didn't attend or graduate from that facility," they would actually drop the conversation and walk away. Many cast judgment on us or doubted our integrity.

At first this bothered me, until one day the Lord told me how to answer if I were asked this question again. He said, "You tell them that you have not graduated from Bible School as you are still in 'His School of Discipleship' and will not receive a diploma until the day you hear the words, 'Well done, thou good and faithful servant.'"

And then it happened. Once again I was asked that same question, to which I replied as I had been instructed. The pastor who asked me the question, this being the second time he asked, stopped upon hearing my response and said,

"You have that correct. That is the most important diploma one could receive." We parted as friends with a clear understanding that receiving those words from God Himself, is more important than any diploma from any school.

(A side note: I am not against Bible schools. In fact, many times I wish that I would have attended one, but God has taught us, and we are glad He has been our teacher.)

We had experienced all this in the past and have overcome, to which we give Him all the glory and honor. But what lay ahead? What was this new anointing He was referring to, and where would we be ministering?

"To everything there is a season..."
(Ecclesiastes 3:1)

I had received an invitation from a pastor in Mexico to teach an Armor Bearer conference in his church. Plans had been made as to the days I would be there, and in preparation, he had done extensive advertising. People were excited, and a large number of people responded.

This conference was happening shortly after "9-11." In fact, it was when I was teaching this conference, that in the middle of the teaching, the Lord spoke to me. I heard Him very clearly as He said, "Turn in your Bible to the book of Amos 8:11-12."

My first thoughts were, "Lord, can't this wait until this conference is over? You know how much time and effort has been put into this teaching, and how important it is that these people need to hear what is being taught." So at first I didn't respond. Then it happened the second time. By now my interpreter was sensing that something was bothering me, so she said, "Brother Roger, what is wrong?"

Still trying to continue on with the teaching, I whispered to her and explained what the Lord had just said. Her response was, "Then Brother Roger, don't you think that is what you should do?" Finally, I surrendered and did what I was instructed to do by the Holy Spirit.

"'Behold, the days are coming,' says the Lord God, 'that I will send a famine on the land, not a famine of bread, nor a thirst for water, but of hearing the words of the Lord. They shall wander from sea to sea, and from north to east; they shall run to and fro, seeking the word of the Lord, but shall find it not.'" (Amos 8:11-12)

"How fitting," I thought. "These verses of scripture are for these people, and they must understand that these words came from Him at that very moment." After sharing these words, I continued on with the conference, which turned out to be well-received by everyone in attendance.

What purpose did this interruption have? That is how I viewed it at the moment it was happening. What lesson was I about to be taught? What mountain would I have to go around or climb again?

It did not end there as my life was about to go through another season.

"To everything there is a season, a time for every purpose under heaven." (Ecclesiastes 3:1)

A few months after "9-11", we began to experience a financial squeeze. Because all our support came from the United States, which was greatly impacted by the "9-11" attack, our funds started to dwindle. In fact, we had reached a decision that we would have to close a resource center for missionaries that we had established in Mission, Texas. The monthly rent had become a huge burden for the ministry.

We were also facing another challenge. God was telling us to close our home in Matehuala, Mexico. Three times we returned to Mexico from the states with the intention of closing our rented home. Three times we returned to the United States having done nothing about it. This was our home away from home, and we had many fond memories of all the ministry that had taken place there. We had our Mexican families who loved us dearly, and we did not want to pluck up what had been planted. (Ecclesiastes 3:2)

What was God trying to teach us? What was He preparing us for? Finally, we made another trip, our fourth one, to bring closure to a home we had fallen in love with. This time we were determined. We kept telling ourselves, "Keep focused. Don't be distracted by what people will be saying." The thought kept running through our minds, "How are we going to dispose of everything we have accumulated?" The answer - we will have a garage sale.

Supernaturally God enabled us to sell everything in our five bedroom home in only two days. We kept one bed and dresser, two night stands, and two lamps, which we moved to the home directly behind ours. This home was being rented by a missionary couple, the Hedges, from Oklahoma. We had become very close friends over the years. Finally, having closed this home and with tears streaming down our cheeks, we headed back to our other home in Mission, Texas.

The financial squeeze that we were feeling as we lived in Mexico, now had tightened its grip on us here in the States. Knowing that God's provision comes in different ways, one of the ways being a secular job, we gave up our home in Texas and returned to Pennsylvania. There I had been promised a job and would be able to start as soon as the relocation was make.

"To everything there is a season, a time for every purpose under heaven." (Ecclesiastes 3:1)

What purpose did all this have in the season of life we were entering into? Upon arrival in Pennsylvania we were greeted and welcomed by our family and friends. It was a time of homecoming. This is where it all had started.

It was a springtime of our lives, a new season, a time to laugh, a time to dance, a time to build up.

Going back to work operating construction equipment was challenging, yet exciting, and it was a source of income. The wages I was being paid soon enabled us to be able to purchase a new manufactured home. This was going to be set up in a park where I was working. My wife spent many hours and days designing every detail of our new home. It would be exactly the way she had planned it, down to the smallest detail.

It finally arrived, and we could hardly wait until it was totally assembled on the lot we had chosen. Having some carpentry skills, I decided that I would build a front and rear deck. This I would do when I was not working, but it needed to be completed prior to our moving in. The decks were important as we would have to walk across them to reach the doors leading into our home.

I would get up before daybreak and go to work on the decks prior to starting my job. Then after working ten to twelve hours, I would hurry home and continue on until my body could take no more.

The day finally arrived when we were able to move in. How beautiful it was, and how proud I was of my wife for the way she had designed our new home.

I continued working long hours and then coming home, night after night, and doing more things outside the home, such as planting the lawn, trees, flowers, building sidewalks and shelves in a newly constructed garage. I was not going to stop until everything was done. I was pushing my body to the limits, and my body was about to respond.

Respond, it did! One morning as I was operating a large piece of construction equipment, I had traveled to a place where there were two twenty-foot sections of twenty-four inch diameter plastic pipe lying in my way. I had the ability to move the two pipes with the piece of equipment, but I decided not to do so for fear of damaging them. I decided I would move them by hand. This would require my climbing down from the equipment and picking up one end and sliding it out of the way.

As I bent down and took hold of the pipe and lifted it, something came over me, something I had never experienced before. Pain immediately started shooting across my chest, and my body broke out in a cold sweat, and breathing became very difficult. In fact, I was gasping for air. Not knowing for sure what had just happened, I knew I somehow had to climb back up onto that piece of equipment and try to make it back to our home which was no more than 2 hundred yards away.

Time after time I tried to climb up onto this piece of equipment. Failing many times, as all my strength was gone from my arms and legs, finally it was as though a hand out of nowhere lifted me up. I was able to move the piece of equipment to a safe parking place and then dismount, which was nothing more than falling off the side. I paused there for a few moments, trying to regain my breath, realizing I must somehow make it back to our home. I recall getting up, walking a few feet, and then having to stop and rest as the pains in my chest were intensifying.

That particular day I was the only person on the jobsite. I had no means of communicating with my boss as I had left my company phone in the house that morning, and there were no neighbors to whom to yell. I knew I had to make it on my own.

Finally, I reached our home. As I entered I headed to the nearest sofa, and on the way, I stopped and picked up our home phone. As I lay there on the sofa, my heart was pounding more rapidly more than ever. The pain had now started shooting across my chest and was traveling down my right side into my arm and hand.

One might wonder where my wife was when all this was happening. Why didn't you contact her for assistance? Months prior, she had received an invitation from an evangelist asking if she would consider accompanying him and our son Duane on a missionary outreach to Ecuador to minister to women. This was the number one desire of her heart, so she responded with a "yes". They had only arrived in Ecuador, at midnight, the night before all this was happening.

Experiencing what I was, I knew I needed medical attention. With the phone in my hand and being led by the Spirit of God, I dialed my neighbor's number. I did it without even knowing their phone number. Within seconds they responded and were in our home and had contacted medical assistance.

Minutes later the police arrived and were followed by the ambulance, which immediately transported me to a local hospital where I was admitted. The hospital had been notified of my arrival and was standing by ready to administer whatever needed to be done. Immediately, after having my vital signs checked, they rushed me to the operating room where I would have to undergo surgery for a badly damaged heart.

As I lay there strapped to the operating table, conscious of all that is going on all around me, I was reminded of what it said in **Ecclesiastes 3:1-2**:

To everything there is a season, a time for every purpose under heaven; a time to be born, and a time to die."

I began to question the Lord. "Lord, I know there are seasons in a person's life when they are born, and a time when they will die. Lord, have I reached that season or time?"

I was introduced to the doctor who would perform the operation. He informed me that the main artery leading to my heart was one hundred percent blocked. The medical team would attempt the procedure where a small balloon device would be inserted into my heart, and if successful, they could open the blockage. He also informed me that they would then attempt to insert a stent to keep the artery open. No guarantees were given, but that was the first step they would attempt.

The doctor asked if I had any questions. I responded with, "Yes, two." First, if he would grant me permission to pray and ask God to direct his hands, and second if it were possible to have a monitor placed so that I could watch the procedure.

He responded with a big "yes" to the first request, and then followed with another "yes" to my second request.

I remember so vividly what happened next. As I closed my eyes for a moment to thank God for watching over me and that the doctor's hands would be guided by the Chief Surgeon, I saw the Lord's hand being extended to me. This was the exact same hand that I had seen when I had visited a church years prior as noted in chapter eight.

I heard Him say, "Just reach out and touch my Hand. That is how close I am to you." Reach out in the position I was in, restrained to the operating table, was impossible in the natural, so I just envisioned reaching out and as I did, the moment our hands met, a peace began to flood my body. It was at this point I gave the doctor permission to begin the procedure.

The surgery was a success as the balloon procedure was successful in opening the blockage. The stent was also implanted into the blocked artery, allowing blood to flow once again through the affected area.

My family had notified my wife in Ecuador about what had happened. I had also sent word that she should remain where she was, that, other than keeping me in prayer, there was nothing more she could do, and the ministry God was about to do through her was going to be awesome.

Praise God for family and friends. My daughter-in-law, Brenda, was constantly at my bedside. The minute I opened my mouth, she was there asking what she could do for me. Family and friends filled my every minute until my wife returned from Ecuador.

Why did God save me from a heart attack which claimed one third of my heart? What was it about this new anointing that He was releasing on my life, that I did not comprehend? Into what season was I about to enter?

"Come to Me, all you who labor and are heavy laden, and I will give you rest." (Matthew 11:28)

I knew I had not taken proper care of my body, and it needed rest, and so I would give it rest. During the weeks ahead, I would spend many hours in His presence. He kept telling me I was in a season of preparation, a time in which He would start to reveal a new course, a new direction we would be traveling. This would also be a time in which my level of confidence would increase as I became saturated with the Word.

"Now this is the confidence that we have in Him, that if we ask anything according to His will, He hears us. And if we know that He hears us, whatever we ask, we know that we have the petitions that we have asked of Him." (I John 5:14-15)

Is this what one can expect if he or she lives his or her life according to the Word? Were the dreams I was experiencing not actually dreams, but a vision of what was about to happen in my life? Could I live my life as one who no longer received his direction from man, but as one who could live his life being directed by a higher order, God Himself?

"To everything there is a season, a time for every purpose under heaven; a time to be born, and a time to die." (Ecclesiastes 3:1-2)

This was not my time to die a physical death, but a time in which I would have to die to self. The more I was willing to die to self, letting go of the comfortable things in life, the more God was going to be able to do through me, in spite of all my shortcomings.

"'No weapon formed against you shall prosper, and every tongue which rises against you in judgment you shall condemn. This is the heritage of the servants of the Lord, and their righteousness is from Me,' says the Lord." (Isaiah 54:17)

The enemy's plan of destruction had been spoiled. The heart attack did not claim my life, but it only made me more determined to walk out His plan, which meant success in whatever I applied my hand.

Questions Only You Can Answer

Chapter 18 "On the Road to a New Season"

Of the four seasons: spring, summer, fall and winter, which one do you like the best?

Why?

Which season do you dislike the most?

Why?

In the seasons mentioned in Ecclesiastes 3:1-8, in which season do you see yourself?

If you are uncomfortable in that season, what plans do you have to move to another season?

Do you agree or disagree with the statement that we are in the midst of a famine of the hearing of the Word of the Lord?

If God were to instruct you to pluck up that which you have planted, what would be the first thing you would put your hand to?

Have you ever been so close to God that you could feel His hand touching yours?

Have you ever had to lie on an operating table knowing that your life was totally in the hands of someone else?

Do you believe one can cause harm to one's body simply by not giving it enough rest?

Do you struggle with dying to self, letting go and letting God have control?

If you answered "yes" to the above question, why?

Are your challenges bigger than the God (god) you serve?

What God (god) do you serve?

Chapter 19

On the Road to Doing the Impossible

"And Jesus said to him, 'If you can believe, all things are possible to him who believes.'"
(Mark 9:23)

What was I believing in? Was I believing in the foolish things of this world, like one could go on sinning, and there would be no consequences? Who was going to be the master of my life?

"No one can serve two masters; for either he will hate the one and love the other, or else he will be loyal to the one and despise the other. You cannot serve God and mammon." (Matthew 6:24)

I was reminded of the promise I had made to the Lord the day I lay on the operating room table after being involved in the truck accident. That day I prayed and said: "Lord, if you take this problem from me, I will serve you the rest of my life." God had not gone back on His promise then, and now He had just rescued me from a life-threatening heart attack.

It was a no-brainer to whom I was going to be loyal. I was committed to serving God.

"And it shall come to pass in the last days, says God, that I will pour out of My Spirit on all flesh: your sons and daughters shall prophesy, your young men shall see visions, your old men shall dream dreams." (Acts 2:17)

It was during the time following the heart attack that the Lord started giving me visions. In fact, they were so real I could actually see different things that were going to happen. I began to journal more and more. I would spend hours writing what God had revealed to me, not always being informed when it would happen, but knowing it would in His timing. This was the seer anointing God had said He was going to release upon my life.

At times it would be so scary that I would have a difficult time trying to comprehend what I had just witnessed. But if God had said: **"So shall My word be that goes forth from My mouth; it shall not return to Me void, but it shall accomplish what I please, and it shall prosper in the thing for which I sent it," (Isaiah 55:11)** then I knew without any shadow of doubt, it was going to happen!

The healing process of my body had moved me into a place that seemed like the starting gate of a horse race. Having spent much time in preparation and training, I saw myself standing there anxiously waiting for the bell to sound. As the bell finally sounded, and the gate swung wide open, my heart leaped, and it was then I realized my attention had to stay focused. It didn't matter who was in front, alongside, or behind me. All I had to do was stay in my lane and keep my eyes focused on the finish line.

**"Then Jesus said to them, 'When you lift up the
Son of Man, then you will know that I am He, and
that I do nothing of Myself; but as My Father
taught Me, I speak these things. And He who sent
Me is with Me. The Father has not left Me alone,
for I always do those things that please Him.'"
(John 8:28-29)**

As I launched out from the starting gate, I did it with the
confidence that God was with me. I had prayed and asked
for boldness, which He had granted. I knew I was being sent
out, but not on my own strength, and I fully understood my
assignment, and His anointing was upon me.

**"How God anointed Jesus of Nazareth with the
Holy Spirit and with power, who went about doing
good and healing all who were oppressed by the
devil, for God was with Him." (Acts10:38)**

It was at this point that I felt like a carpenter who had
gathered up all his tools, along with the blueprint in his hand,
and was headed out to work. A carpenter must be able to read
(see) and understand a blueprint, if it is to be of any significance to him in accomplishing the task set before him.

I had my tools, the Word and my blueprint, the visions
which God had revealed to me. Excitement was racing
through my body. It was there, the same feelings I had experienced whenever I had started a new job. I had confidence,
and I was ready to tackle any job He had for me.

**"Then Jesus answered and said to them, 'Most
assuredly, I say to you, the Son can do nothing
of Himself, but what He sees the Father do;
for whatever He does, the Son also does in like
manner. For the Father loves the Son, and shows**

Him all things that He Himself does; and He will show Him greater works than these. that you may marvel."' (John 5:19-20)

God had gone before me and set up the work sites.

I want to re-emphasize that whenever I write about doing ministry, it always includes my wife, Nancy, as well. God had supernaturally brought us together, and we have always ministered as a team. As we stepped out and began to minister the Word with power and authority, the supernatural started happening. Wherever we ministered, people were falling to their knees and repenting and asking Jesus into their hearts. People were being set free from lifetime bondages which had held them captive, and we began seeing miracle after miracle as we prayed for the sick and laid hands on them as He had commanded.

"While Peter was still speaking these words, the Holy Spirit fell upon all those who heard the word." (Acts 10:44)

This is what was happening as the Holy Spirit moved throughout every meeting and place of ministry. God began moving us from place to place, as we were not to settle in one particular place. Wherever He sent us in Mexico or in the United States, there we were met by people who had needs, and God was going to meet their needs.

It was on one of our journeys in the United States that we were invited by Larry and Karen Hostetter, our faithful prayer partners for over eighteen years, to attend a meeting with them. It was on a Saturday morning and at a time when our schedules would allow us this free time. We knew nothing about this meeting other than its name.

Upon arriving at the location where the meeting was to be held, we were introduced to the brother in charge of the ministry there. He was the man who ministered the Word that morning. This was all we knew about this man, or the ministry in which he operated.

"And He Himself gave some to be apostles, some prophets, some evangelists, and some pastors and teachers." (Ephesians 4:11)

This brother flowed in the prophetic. I had heard prophets speak before, but many times after hearing what they said, I ended up in a state of confusion or doubt. For example, I was attending a service when a man stood up and said, "In row thirteen, there are four people who will be getting a new home in the next twelve months." In my opinion that was not a word of prophecy but a generic word, as there may have been thirty people seated in row thirteen. That to me was the law of averages and not a word from the Lord. Like I mentioned before, this is only in my opinion.

It is my belief that a true prophetic word from the Lord, coming through man, will confirm what has already been deposited into your spirit. Furthermore, it will be confirmed by two or three witnesses.

As the brother started to talk, it was as though he had a book in front of him, and he was reading it aloud. This book contained information that only God, Nancy, and I knew about. It was confirmation of what had happened in the past and our heart for the future and a lot more.

The following, in quotations, are actual excerpts taken from the word spoken over us:

Brother: "Roger and Nancy, they came from Texas. What do you do in Texas?"

Roger: "We're both in ministry. We've been working in Mexico for seventeen years."

Brother: "What is it you do in ministry?"

Roger: "We teach leadership basically. We believe that you have to equip people for the work of the ministry. God has called us to make disciples. I can't find anywhere where it says we have to go out and do all the work. (This was because we were called to equip others to do the work of ministry.) That's our heart."

Brother: "What are you doing here? You are raising up people. That is part of the process."

"When you guys came in, it's amazing, but you have several anointings on your life, several, like different hats that you wear at different times that the Lord has you in. I saw a whole thing of hats. It's almost like it is strapped on your back, and every so often, you take the one out and put it on, then put the other one back again, then put the other one on or whatever.

"I hear the Lord say this, Roger and Nancy. 'I have called you especially for this time. Oh, I've chosen you, and I've spoken to you many times, and the relationship that I have with you is an awesome relationship.' I hear Him saying: 'I look forward when you come to Me. I listen for your footsteps when you come to pray with Me, and you come to listen to what I have to say. Oh yeah, there sometimes is a stubbornness in you. There is a stubbornness in you, because sometimes I've told you to do something, and you just went ahead and did it your way. You saw it wasn't right and went back and got on the right track again, but I've chosen you, and I've called you, and I've anointed you with My end-time, it's a prophetic teaching, prophetic teachers, to prophesy and to go forth and to teach the Word with a great anointing.'

"I see this. I hear this right now: 'You are the ones I have chosen, because you don't like to compromise the Word of God, and because you have chosen to speak the truth of My Word, there will be an even greater anointing that will come upon you and those desires of your heart, I see in both of you.'

"I hear the Lord say this: 'You have said to Me, "Oh Lord, I want to see more healings take place. I want to see it, Lord. It's the desire of my heart, Lord. I see these people hurting, Lord, and I hear these things here and here, but Lord, it's my desire and my heart's desire, Lord. We want to do it. We want to lay hands on the sick, and we want to see them recover. Lord, that's the desire of our hearts.'

"Roger, the Lord would say unto you: 'You're going to see it before you leave this earth. You and Nancy will see some of the greatest miracles that will ever have taken place.' And it will come as you begin to do what the Lord says, He asks you to do in obedience to Him. But you will begin to see, for the Lord says, 'There is something that is going to come out of heaven in 1- 2- 3- 4- 5- 6 months from now. Six months from now, a supernatural anointing, that is coming from heaven, and when it hits both of you, and it will hit both of you at the same time, that you will be changed into almost like you won't believe how the change is going to take place. Your thinking is going to change, a spirit of might and a spirit of counsel that is coming upon you, and you are going to have supernatural wisdom, and the seer anointing with a greater ability to see.'"

Nancy and I sat there in total amazement as we knew this was from God. There was no way possible for this man, whom we met for the first time that day, to know these things pertaining to our lives, unless God had revealed them to him as he spoke.

He then invited me to come forward and share from my heart, after which he continued on for a total of twenty-three minutes as he spoke many words which not only were words of confirmation, but words of guidance as well.

I had mentioned earlier in this chapter that I believe a true prophetic word from the Lord, coming through man, will confirm what has already been deposited into your spirit. This was definitely confirmation, but what was going to happen in six months, and where would this place be?

After attending this meeting, we headed back to Texas and then into Mexico to continue ministering the Word. It was then that I was approached by one of our pastors and asked if I would be the main speaker at a Salvation and Healing Crusade which they were planning on hosting. Without saying I would pray and ask God if this is what He wanted me to do, I responded with a big "yes".

The date and place had already been arranged as preparations were under way. This crusade was to be held in a ranch about thirty minutes south of where we were staying in Matehuala. A ranch, as they are referred to, is a group of homes ranging in number from three to a hundred homes and is located outside a city's boundaries. This ranch was a typical ranch having thirty to forty homes, a couple of stores which sold sodas, chips, and snacks, and a soccer field with no seating, electric services, or bathroom facilities on site.

A lot of work had to be done in preparation for this crusade at the soccer field. A portable stage area was erected, generators were rented to furnish the necessary power to run the sound equipment, and chairs were also rented and transported to this area. Once these items were delivered and set up, we had to have twenty-four hour a day security to insure our investment. People from our church took shifts guarding the equipment and at night, they would actually sleep on the site.

The day finally came for the crusade to begin. The people were excited as there had been much prayer, fasting, and advertising done prior to this time. A local group of musicians had been hired, and they led praise and worship which continued for over ninety minutes.

Then came the time for the delivery of God's Word, which was followed by an invitation for anyone desiring to ask Jesus into their hearts. Many people, young and old, came forward and confessed Jesus as their Lord and Savior.

It was at this crusade that I ministered the Word concerning healing. To the day, this was six months from the day when the brother in the service in Lancaster, Pennsylvania had prophesied this would happen.

"And when He had called His twelve disciples to Him, He gave them power over unclean spirits, to cast them out, and to heal all kinds of sickness and all kinds of disease." (Matthew 10:1)

"And these signs will follow those who believe: In My name they will cast out demons; they will speak with new tongues; they will take up serpents; and if they drink anything deadly, it will by no means hurt them; they will lay hands on the sick, and they will recover." (Mark 16:17-18)

As the invitation for physical and emotional healing was given, people began to flood to the altar area. They had come expecting to receive from God, and nothing was going to stop them. Men, women, and children of all ages responded to the invitation. I proceeded to receive and give forth words of knowledge concerning healings.

"Now there is in Jerusalem by the Sheep Gate a pool, which is called in Hebrew, Bethesda, (Bethesda literally means 'Place of Outpouring') having five porches. In these lay a great multitude of sick people, blind, lame, paralyzed, waiting for the moving of the water. For an angel went down at a certain time into the pool and stirred up the water; then whoever stepped in first, after the stirring of the water, was made well of whatever disease he had.

"Now a certain man was there who had an infirmity for thirty-eight years. When Jesus saw him lying there, and knew that he already had been in that condition a long time, He said to him, 'Do you want to be made well?'

"The sick man answered Him, 'Sir, I have no man to put me into the pool when the water is stirred up; but while I am coming, another steps down before me.'

"Jesus said to him, 'Rise, take up your bed and walk.' And immediately the man was made well, took up his bed, and walked..." (John 5:2-9)

We were at the right place, the place of His outpouring, and the waters were stirred. Nancy began to minister to people with all types of afflictions, accompanied by the laying on of hands. People with leg and knee problems walked away totally healed and relieved from years of pain and suffering. Shoulder, back, and neck ailments were totally healed. A man with a chronic heart condition, scheduled for surgery, was prayed for and totally healed.

It was during the time of laying hands on people and praying for them, that I was led to a woman who had come forward. Normally, we would ask them what it was they wanted us to agree with them for God to do in their lives.

However this time, the normal was about to change. What I was about to say to her had never happened to me before. My words to her before she could say a thing were this, "The Lord said He was not going to heal your body tonight, that you have sin in your life, which you need to deal with first." I continued to tell her that she was living with a man who was not her husband, and this was what would prevent her from receiving her healing. I will never forget the look on this woman's face as she looked me directly in the eye and said, "How do you know that?"

I informed her, "It's through the Holy Spirit that God revealed these things to me." Her head dropped, as tears began to stream down her cheeks. A moment later, she went on to tell me that was the truth, and since I had never met this woman before, she was convinced I had heard from God. I did not pray for that woman that night, as the Holy Spirit instructed me.

Special note: This woman came back the next night and shared this testimony of what happened. When she returned home that night, she discovered a note on her kitchen table from the man she had allowed to live with her. In it he stated that he could no longer live there and was returning home to his wife and children. That same night after sharing what had happened, she repented before God, was prayed for, and received her healing. To God be the glory!

Minutes before the start of the second night of the crusade, the weather decided it did not want to cooperate with us. We could see rain clouds off in the distance, moving very rapidly in our direction. As the musicians were about to take their place on the platform, it began to rain. Since this was an open-air crusade with no provision for protection from the rain, everything had to be put on hold.

As people headed to their vehicles to get out of the rain, a few of us decided we had better stay right there and begin to pray for God to intervene. I recall a man who had been hired to videotape the services standing there with us. This man was not a believer, although he had heard the message the night before. We cried out to the Lord, and He responded. As fast as the storm had moved in, it moved out. Within minutes we were standing in the dry and able to proceed with the crusade. That man said, "Even the rain clouds respond to their prayers." Later in the service, he accepted Jesus as his Lord and Savior and the following night, he also brought his wife and family, who all followed in his footsteps.

The waters had been stirred, and unlike the man at the pool of Bethesda, it would not only be the first person to enter the water who would receive his healing, but everyone who took that step of faith.

The crusade continued on for a total of four nights, with many signs and wonders happening.

"And it shall come to pass in the last days, says God, that I will pour out of My Spirit on all flesh..." (Acts 2:17a)

Just as it was written, God poured out of His Spirit upon all flesh. He had not emptied Himself, but had merely given of Himself to all those who would receive. God was relying on us to be His mouthpiece and His extended hands.

How could all this be happening? What was it God had in store for this grandma and grandpa? Did He forget we were just ordinary people who had not graduated from any college and had no degrees?

Having come this far in life, I knew the direction my feet were to take. The book of Acts had become a pathway upon which I had been directed to walk. The book of Acts is also the story of the disciples receiving what Jesus received in order to do what Jesus did.

**"Then Peter opened his mouth and said: 'In truth I perceive that God shows no partiality.'"
(Acts 10:34)**

That being the case, that God shows no partiality, then the disciples receiving what Jesus received in order to do what Jesus did, was part of the anointing upon our lives. God had set us up, and we were "on the road to doing greater works."

Chapter 19 "On the Road to Doing the Impossible"

Who is master of your life, God or mammon?

Do you believe in prophecy?

Has a prophet ever prophesied over you confirming what had already been deposited in your spirit?

Do you believe that every word that proceeds from the mouth of God shall not return void to Him?

Do you understand that as God spoke to men in times past, they penned His Word and recorded it in what today is known as the Bible?

Do you experience times of stubbornness when you only want to do things your way?

Do you or someone near to you recognize a special anointing on your life?

What, if anything, have you done with His anointing?

Do you exercise the power over unclean spirits and sickness and disease that you have as a disciple of God?

Have you ever been under the spigot of "His Place of Outpouring"?

Do you believe in the "laying on of hands" for healing of the afflicted?

Do you believe that since Jesus has returned to heaven to be with the Father that we have been ordained to do His will here on earth?

Presently, what are you struggling with that's keeping you from doing His Word and praying for the sick?

Chapter 20

On the Road to Doing Greater Works

"Most assuredly, I say to you, he who believes
in Me, the works that I do he will do also; and
greater works than these he will do, because I go
to My Father. And whatever you ask in My name,
that I will do, that the Father may be glorified in
the Son. If you ask anything in My name, I will do
it." (John 14:12-14)

Nancy and I had an understanding of what these verses
of scripture were saying, since Jesus Christ had gone
to be with the Father, we knew our work had been cut out
for us.

We realized that a vital key to walking in the pathway of
God's miracles was to stay available to His leading. We were
aware that when blessings started coming our way, it would
be tempting to be content thinking that was all God had for
us, and find it easy to lie back, relax, and take our hands from
the plow.

The cost of discipleship:

"But Jesus said to him, 'No one, having put his hand to the plow. and looking back, is fit for the kingdom of God.'" (Luke 9:62)

God was not going to allow us to half-heartedly serve Him. He demanded our undivided attention, and there was to be no turning or looking back. He was not calling us to attempt to produce more, but to ask and believe Him for more. He had greater works in store for us. All we had to do was receive, and, by His grace, achieve for His Kingdom purposes and glory. God began to prepare our hearts to do greater works than we had ever been assigned before.

During the fall of 2007 we traveled and ministered in a number of churches in Pennsylvania. It was during this time that the Lord gave me a vision of a church. It was so clear and defined that I knew every detail about this church building. Nancy, knowing about this vision, as I had explained it to her, knew I would not rest until I found out where it was located. She had experienced and been around me before when God had given me a vision.

We had discussed the possibilities of where it could possibly be located and came up with the idea it might be in a neighboring town, which we were both familiar with. Determined to find this building, I set out on a journey, driving up and down every street in that town.

As I came around a corner, my eyes fell on the answer. There it was. Then to my disappointment, as I took a closer look, this was not the one God had shown me. I continued on driving up and down the many streets of that town. I was determined. Nothing was going to stop me, and then all of a sudden, I heard the Lord say, "Drive south on Route 495." Immediately, I headed in that direction and after traveling a few miles, I heard Him say, "Turn around. You have gone too far." My first reaction was, "Lord, you're playing games with me." There was no church on that road, that I saw. However, I did turn around and head back to the town from which I had just come.

As I was driving back and just about in the middle of an intersection, I heard Him say, "Turn left." Unable to make the left turn due to oncoming traffic, I drove two blocks more and pulled into a mall to do a U-turn. There I noticed a few men doing some unique landscaping, so I paused and observed them for a few minutes prior to continuing on my journey. Being back on course, I drove to the intersection and turned, as I had been told. After only traveling two hundred feet, I heard Him say, "Turn Right" and in doing so, I found myself headed up what seemed like a private driveway.

As I traveled up this road, I eventually come to a church building. "Lord, what is this all about?" I shouted out. This was by no means the one He had shown me in the vision. By now, confusion had entered my mind. Did I really hear God speak to me when He directed me to this place? Where do I go from here? I paused for a few minutes reading the information posted on the church directory and finally decided it was time to head back home.

As I drove back down the driveway, I came to a stop sign where I would have to make a left turn, enabling me to return the way I had come. As I waited there, a car came from my right, which had its left turn signal on, indicating the person wanted to make a left turn onto the driveway on which I was now parked. Deciding not to pull out in front of this vehicle, I waited until he made the turn and in doing so, he stopped next to me.

As both of us rolled down our windows, this man proceeded to ask me what I was doing there, and how he could help me. He was the pastor of that church. My answer was very simply, "I really don't know." We spoke for about ten minutes and in that time, I had shared the vision God had given me of a church building, and I acknowledged that it was definitely not his building. However, it was in our time of conversation that God had given me a word for this man. It was a word in season, for which he acknowledged and thanked me. He said, if for no other reason than to have that word spoken over him, then that was the reason why God had me there at that very precise moment.

As I drove away from that divine meeting, I began to thank God for His faithfulness. I thanked Him for the word He had dropped in my spirit, and how He knew what this man needed to hear, and when he needed to hear it.

But I still had an unanswered question, "Where is that church building He had shown me?" Not hearing any other directions, I drove on to search out another city. Something was compelling me to head to the southernmost part of this city. In doing so I came to one of the most beautiful sights my eyes could behold. There it was. The circular driveway leading up to the entrance of the church was exactly as I had seen. The front door, the roof lines were all in their proper places. The cross on the front of the building - my heart skipped a beat, it was not in the right place. In the vision God had given me, the cross was on the front of the building and on this building it was up on the roof. How close to being the right one, but close to being the right one was not the answer.

I decided it was time to return to where my wife was working. At this time Nancy was working at a well-known local fruit and produce stand. The owners were people who loved the Lord and ones Nancy felt very comfortable with and had the freedom with whom to share her heart.

Earlier that day Nancy had shared the vision with the woman who owned the business. She did not immediately respond with any comments, but later returned with a pencil drawing of a church building which she gave to Nancy and said, "Have Roger check this out. It might be the one he is searching for."

As I arrived there, my wife could hardly wait to see my response as she handed me the drawing. As I took one look, I said, "This could very possibly be the one." It looked like the one, but I was not going to be sure until I saw it with my own eyes.

The next morning, after driving my wife back to her place of employment, I headed out in the direction of this church. As I pulled up in front of it, I knew that I knew I this was the building had shown me. Everything! Everything was exactly as God had shown me! No second guessing of having to settle for almost. It was exact in every detail.

I could not believe my eyes and was excited as I walked up to the front door. To my surprise the front door was locked. I assumed someone was there, because there was a vehicle parked in the driveway with no one in it. Surely the pastor must be there. I looked for a doorbell, but there was none to be found. As I stood there peering into the foyer of the church, I noticed someone walk by. This person must have noticed me, so he then made his way to the front door to greet me.

After explaining to him why I was there, he said I should speak directly to the pastor, that he was a maintenance man who was cleaning the building. He gave me the pastor's cell phone number and encouraged me to give him a call. God's timing never ceases to amaze me. It had to have been God who directed this man to be walking down this hallway at the precise moment in time that I was standing at the door.

Within a few minutes after thanking the man for letting me in, I was on the phone, calling the pastor of the church. When I spoke to the pastor, he informed me that the maintenance man had already phoned him, and he wanted to know more about the vision and when we could meet.

The next day we met and talked for over two hours at which time he asked me if I would minister in his church the following Sunday. Although we had made plans to start our journey back to Texas before that particular Sunday, I said yes, we would alter our plans. Immediately following that Sunday service, we headed back to Texas

Fall in eastern Pennsylvania is a beautiful sight. It is a season of change as the leaves turn from their summer green to awesome colors of red, yellow, and brown. Fall also proceeds winter, when once again things of nature go through a dramatic change. Trees lose their leaves and go into a state of dormancy. It is a time of rest, a time of preparation for the upcoming season.

Being back in Texas was for us was like the winter season in Pennsylvania. We needed time to relax and time to prepare for the future. We knew that unless our minds were alert and our bodies refreshed, we could not be as effective as God wanted us to be.

We were positive that He would reveal to us our next assignment. Little by little, He started to unveil His plan for our lives. We were to go to Pennsylvania and hold a two day crusade, which was to be named "Winds of Change Healing Outpouring." The date was next, as He disclosed July 12 and 13, 2008, but somehow He forgot to tell me the exact location.

With our living in Texas at that time, and my son, Duane, having just moved back to Pennsylvania from Texas, was my answer. I contacted him and asked him to search for a place in which we could hold this meeting.

Much to my surprise, what he found in the range of seating capacity that I had suggested, would run anywhere from 15 hundred to 6 thousand dollars per night. In some cases this did not include a raised stage area, which would be an additional expense. We also would have to rent sound equipment. All these expenses had put this out-of-sight for us. Since it was already the middle of March by this time, I knew I needed answers, and I needed them soon, as July was quickly approaching, and there was a lot of preparation that needed to be done.

My next thought was to telephone some pastors in that area to see if they knew of anything more reasonable. One of the first pastors I phoned was the pastor of the church God had led me to on our previous journey to Pennsylvania. I explained to him what I was searching for, and he said he had no knowledge of any such rental place. I decided I would continue praying and asking God to reveal the place.

That night as I was sleeping, the Lord gave me a vision. In this vision I saw a nursing home located not too many miles from where the church was that God had directed me to the previous year. I recognized the nursing home, due to the fact I had at one time worked in that area. In the vision I saw, backed up to the nursing home entrance, two vans with people being escorted into them. Then the vans pulled out of the driveway, and they were "on the road to ... ?" Where were these vans headed to? I saw it all unfold before my very eyes. It was like I was in the van with them. Finally, they reached their destination. Much to my surprise, it was at the church I saw in the vision in 2007, and the one in which I had ministered.

Lord, could this be the answer? Is there where we are to hold the "Winds Of Change Healing Outpouring?" Lord, You know just yesterday I spoke to the pastor, and he didn't mention anything of possibly using his facility.

"Casting all your care upon Him, for He cares for you." (I Peter 5:7)

That night, before going to bed, I had cast the care of a place to hold the crusade upon Him. But now I was facing another challenge. Did I expect God to remove my anxiety, since He was the one who had just revealed these things to me in a vision? I was too keyed up to sleep, and what had started out to be a peaceful night's rest, now had me up pacing the floor.

Late that morning, as my mind was searching for possible answers, I decided I would call another pastor whom I knew. This pastor had held events before, and I knew if anyone could help, he would be the one. As I went to call him, I realized that his number was one I had lost when my wife accidentally dropped my phone into a kitchen sink full of water.

No problem, I thought. I'll call the pastor to whom I had spoken yesterday, for I knew the two of them were friends and for sure he would have the number. As the phone rang, I heard a voice answer and say, "Good morning, Bro. Roger. How are you today?" (Caller ID had informed him who was calling.)

"Great," I responded and went on to say, "You will not believe what happened last night." Before I could go any further, he interrupted me and said, "I have something I must tell you. Last night the Lord spoke to me and said we are to let you use our facility, without charge, for the first two nights of the 'Winds of Change Healing Outpouring.'"

"Praise the Lord!" I shouted, and then I commenced to tell him about the vision God had given me. God had just confirmed to both of us that this was the place He wanted us to use.

A few days later as the pastor and I were talking, he said that the church board had unanimously decided that they would allow the meetings to continue on as long as the Lord would direct. The first two nights would be the responsibility of Operation-A-Vision "Winds of Change Healing Outpouring." After that everything would then become the responsibility of the church. The board also extended an invitation, asking if I would remain as long as needed and be one of the main speakers.

I agreed to all the terms set before me and was now ready to tackle all the necessary plans for the upcoming outpouring.

Contact was made with a brother who graciously accepted the responsibility of leading praise and worship. We were kept busy writing newspaper advertisements, designing posters, writing personal letters of invitation, making phone calls, and asking volunteers for their assistance.

"For the kingdom of heaven is like a man traveling to a far country, who called his own servants and delivered his goods to them. And to one he gave five talents, to another two, and to another one, to each according to his own ability; and immediately he went on a journey.

"Then he who had received the five talents went and traded with them, and made another five talents. And likewise he who had received two gained two more also. But he who had received one went and dug in the ground, and hid his lord's money.

"After a long time the lord of those servants came and settled accounts with them. So he who had received five talents came and brought five other talents, saying, 'Lord, you delivered to me five talents; look, I have gained five more talents besides them.'

"His lord said to him, 'Well done, good and faithful servant; you were faithful over a few things, I will make you ruler over many things. Enter into the joy of your lord.'

"He also who had received two talents came and said, 'Lord, you delivered to me two talents; look, I have gained two more talents besides them.'

"His lord said to him, 'Well done, good and faithful servant; you have been faithful over a few things, I will make you ruler over many things. Enter into the joy of your lord.'

"Then he who had received the one talent came and said, 'Lord, I knew you to be a hard man, reaping where you have not sown, and gathering where you have not scattered seed. And I was afraid, and went and hid your talent in the ground. Look, there you have what is yours.'

"But his lord answered and said to him, 'You wicked and lazy servant, you knew that I reap where I have not sown, and gather where I have not scattered seed. So you ought to have deposited my money with the bankers, and at my coming I would have received back my own with interest. Therefore take the talent from him, and give it to him who has ten talents. For to everyone who has, more will be given, and he will have abundance; but from him who does not have, even what he has will be taken away. And cast the unprofitable servant into the outer darkness. There will be weeping and gnashing of teeth.'"
(Matthew 25:14-30)

Plans were underway for the outpouring, and we decided to make one last trip into Mexico to visit our two churches. God had given us much, and we had to do something. Doing nothing was like the person who received the one talent. We understood that the wise use of our gifts and abilities entrusted to us would result in great opportunities, while their neglect would result, not only in the loss of opportunities, but also loss of what had been entrusted to us.

Upon arrival in Mexico, invitations to minister the Word began coming in one after another. We ministered in our two churches numerous times and also in the ranch where the crusade had been held. We also traveled another six hours south from Matehuala to cities near Mexico City, where we had awesome services. God's presence, His Spirit, was present in every service, and we witnessed miracle after miracle as we laid hands on people for physical and spiritual healing.

One night back in our hometown of Matehuala, Mexico, as Nancy was ministering the Word, she gave an invitation for anyone having a physical need to come forward, and she would lay hands on them, releasing the healing power of God into their bodies.

There was a young boy there whom we had come to know. This sixteen year old boy was suffering with Down Syndrome. He had come forward many times for healing, and each time hands were laid on him, he would throw himself on the concrete floor and just lay there with a big smile on his face.

This night was no different as the same actions followed as hands were laid on him. As he lay there, I felt compassion starting to rise up in me. In fact, it became so strong that before I knew what was happening, I found myself kneeling next to him with my hand on his chest.

What was happening? Why was I experiencing what I was? Why was tonight so different than any other night? Where was my level of faith? We had seen so many miracles: blind eyes opened, lame people walking, deaf people receiving their hearing, chronic diseases being healed, broken relationships being restored, but never a person with Down Syndrome healed. Was tonight going to be a breakthrough?

The boy was lying there in a prone position and was motionless. His eyes were fixed, staring toward heaven. Something was happening as I heard the Lord say, "Start praying the Blood of Jesus over him and say nothing other than the name of Jesus."

Every time I would say the name of "Jesus", this boy would actually levitate, his body coming off the floor, and then with my hand on his chest, I would literally push him back on the floor. This continued on for almost twenty minutes. Then something happened, which actually scared me. As I was watching his facial expression throughout this entire ordeal, I now noticed that his tongue had swollen to a point that it filled his entire mouth. His body started convulsing very rapidly, and the levitation also increased.

The more I spoke the name "Jesus", it seemed the worse things were getting. That was until he went completely limp and lay there barely breathing. In fact, his breathing had gotten to a point where I checked his pulse to see if he were still alive. I watched as slowly his tongue returned to normal size, and then he opened his eyes. He kept staring at me as to say, "What happened?"

"And these signs will follow those who believe: In My name they will cast out demons ..."
(Mark 16:17)

What had him bound was broken, and he was set free. He was set free to the point where he began to repeat the words I would say to him. "Thank you Jesus," were the first words this sixteen year old boy had ever spoken!

We concluded our ministry time in Mexico, and then returned to our home in Alamo, Texas. Once back in the sates, we received more invitations to minister the Word in local churches, which we gladly accepted.

Our journey back to Pennsylvania was on schedule, and everything was falling in place. We had received an invitation to attend and speak at a missions' conference in Portland, Texas prior to heading back to the east coast. This was the first missions' conference this church had ever hosted. The pastor and his staff put out the red carpet for all the missionaries who attended. Everything was done with excellence.

Due to a guest speaker becoming ill and being unable to speak at his designated time, a switch in scheduling had to be made. Originally I had been scheduled to share a ministry time with a fellow missionary, but due to the schedule change, I was given the entire Sunday evening service. Once again as the name of Jesus was proclaimed, we witnessed many miracles and the moving of His Holy Spirit.

Still having time before we had to start our journey back to Pennsylvania, we headed west to Seiling, Oklahoma. Our friends, Darwin and Laverne Hedges, had spoken to their pastor, and he had extended an invitation for us to come and minister the word to his congregation. God, being omnipresent, set the scene for an outpouring of His Healing power in that church. It was an awesome weekend. We were totally blessed by everyone who attended. God had truly made a divine connection through our visit.

Finally, we were on our way, heading east to our next assignment, "Winds of Change Healing Outpouring". On the evening of July 11th all those who would assist in the "Outpouring" joined us for a time of final instructions and corporate prayer. Wow, what a night as God's presence filled the temple, and His Glory shone round about.

All the preparation and times of prayer were about to be put to the test. July 12th came and as it did, everyone in the service felt His presence. All who came to the "Outpouring" came with the expectancy of receiving from God, and God was not about to fail any. Many lives were changed as they prayed and asked Jesus to wash away their sins and to become Lord of their lives. This was the beginning, and not the end, of what God was going to do.

As the Word was taught, people were asked: Are you sick? Have you received a bad report? Come receive your healing through the proclamation of words of knowledge, the Word of God, the prayer of faith, and the laying on of hands.

> **"Most assuredly, I say to you, he who believes in Me, the works that I do he will do also; and greater works than these he will do, because I go to My Father. And whatever you ask in My name, that I will do, that the Father may be glorified in the Son. If you ask anything in My name, I will do it." (John 14:12-14)**

This is what we had been commissioned to do. The first two nights were history, and now the board was faced with the decision to either stop or continue on. They were in one accord and unanimously decided to continue with nightly meetings. With everything in place, the church was committed to allow the meetings to continue on, giving opportunity for the **"pouring out of His Spirit upon all flesh." (Acts 2:17)**

After ministering fifteen continuous nightly meetings, it was decided to go to four nights per week. Many of the volunteers worked full-time daily jobs, and fatigue was starting to set in.

In the first seventy-three days, we had held fifty services. We didn't stop after the first seventy-three days, but continued on ministering the Word for almost six months. We had prayed for revival, and we were witnessing many lives being transformed.

I stop at this point in time and reflect back on all those faithful people whom God had brought to our side. How could we have done all we had without their help and support. A huge "thank you" to all!

Was this assignment over? Were things coming to an end? During this assignment God had led us to begin leadership classes at this church. Nancy and I are firm believers in training leaders to make a difference, and we had agreed to teach leadership principles to this group of people. Not only did we present them with leadership material, we also challenged the team coaches to write their vision statement concerning the team they would be leading.

It was during this time of leadership training that I received invitations from two churches in Texas to minister the Word. We needed a break from teaching, so we planned to fly back to Texas to minister God's Word. The Holy Spirit moved in the services at both churches, and many people responded to the invitations that were given.

Some weeks prior to leaving Pennsylvania for this time in Texas as I was praying, God revealed some things to me in a vision. He had shown me three different healings that were going to manifested in a service, but He did not tell me when or where. I saw them in detail. The first healing was: Jesus put His hands in the form of a circle and placed them on a person's damaged knee and simply spoke the words, "Be healed in the name of Jesus."

The second was Jesus laying His hands on a person who had very limited motion in their shoulder and saying the words, "Be healed in the name of Jesus."

The third was that there would be a person in attendance who had been involved in an automobile accident and had had whiplash, which in turn had damaged their third and fourth vertebrae. These instructions were very precise.

After delivering the word which I had entitled, "Daily Living Your Life as They Did in the Book of Acts" in the second church which was located in Portland, Texas, I gave an invitation for anyone who needed a special touch to come forward and receive what the Lord had promised in His Word. Many people responded, and God was about to do the supernatural. It was while Nancy and others whom we had anointed for healing were praying for people, that I sensed God saying, "Today is the day."

When I said, "God wants to heal a person with a knee problem," two women came forward and said, "That's me." With that, I called for Nancy to come and pray for these women. As she approached these women, she grabbed the pastor's twelve year-old daughter, and they together formed their hands into a circle, and they placed them on these women's knees and spoke the words, "Be healed in the name of Jesus." Instantly these women received their healings. It was later that Nancy revealed to me that the pastor, the twelve year-old girl's father, had prophesied over his daughter two weeks before the healing service, that God was going to use her to do unusual things at her young age.

Next, I revealed what the Lord had shown me about the person who had been in an auto accident, had suffered whip-lash, and had a damaged third and fourth vertebrae. At first no one responded. Finally a woman came forward and said, "That is me." Hands were laid on this woman who responded with, "I feel much different."

Then I said about the person with a torn rotator-cuff. Two people immediately responded with a third person following. The one was a man who was in pain, unable to lift his arm further than shoulder high. The other was a woman who was ecstatic, screaming, "I am healed! I am healed! I am not going to be denied. I am healed!"

God's Word was in operation as we witnessed many miracles. After the conclusion of that service, Nancy and I returned back to our home in Alamo, Texas.

The following Sunday, I called the pastor's wife and prayed for her as she would be ministering the Word that morning in place of her husband, who was still out of the country on a mission's trip. It is always great to receive words of encouragement. On Sunday evening, my wife decided to call the pastor's wife to see how the morning service had gone. This was her report of what had been shared in the morning service: 1) the women with the damaged knees both were walking pain free; 2) the woman with the whiplash was able to do things she had not done since the accident, which had happened thirty-five years prior; 3) the man who had a damaged rotator-cuff and was unable to sleep with his wife due to the fact that her turning in bed would irritate the afflicted area, was now able to once again sleep with his wife; 4) the other woman gave testimony that she had no pain when trying to comb her hair. They all gave glory to God for their healings.

It was time to fly back to Pennsylvania and resume our leadership teaching responsibilities. When we returned there, we were greeted by a classroom full of hungry people. Something was welling up inside of them, and they were eager to know more. Who were these men and women?

"And He Himself gave some to be apostles, some prophets, some evangelists, and some pastors and teachers." (Ephesians 4:11)

What was happening in each of their lives? Why had they committed to do what they were doing?

"For the equipping of the saints for the work of ministry, for the edifying of the body of Christ." (Ephesians 4:12)

These were the people who had received a calling from God and had responded with a big "yes".

Another season in our lives was coming to an end. The time had come, and we knew it was time to head back to our home in Texas, but not before we had a time of recognizing all the teams, their coaches, and assistants. It was amazing how God had revived these people. As they stood and formed a line which stretched from one end of the stage to the other, it became evident these were God's chosen people.

When we first returned to Pennsylvania, we only had made plans of being there for the two nights of "Winds of Change Healing Outpouring" services. The pastor of that church, to which God had directed us, provided us with a place to live for almost six months. He and his wife and family, as well as his congregation were such a blessing to us and made us feel as though we were part of their family. We cannot express enough our heartfelt gratitude to those people.

Saying our farewells was not easy as we headed out on our two thousand mile journey back to Texas. We left with tears in our eyes, tear of sadness, due to the fact that we had to leave our own family and old and new friends once again. Our tears were also tears of joy, the joy that only comes from doing the will of the Father. What a blessing it will be to hear the words, "Well done, good and faithful servant."

These thoughts filled our minds as we headed out "on the road to ... ?" knowing one thing, that life is not a destination. It's a journey, and God is in the details.

Questions Only You Can Answer

Chapter 20 "On the Road to Doing Greater Works"

If life is a journey, and God is into details, has He revealed to you His plan for your life?

Do you know that you know, on which road you are to travel?

Have you ever gone fishing and done any casting?

When a person "casts", he releases the object, and it has the liberty to travel, unrestricted, unless a brake is applied. If we are to **"cast our cares upon Him for He cares for us,"** and we are the ones who have the ability to apply the brake, then what do you find yourself holding on to, unable to release?

Are you a person who is as good as your word, so that people know your "yes" is "yes" and your "no" is "no"?

Do you see yourself as a five, two, or one talent person?

What have you done with the talents entrusted to you?

Are you fully aware of the consequences a person will have to suffer for the misuse of his/her talents?

Do you believe God's healing power is present for you this day?

Have you ever been in a service when God's healing power filled the place, and you witnessed the supernatural?

What is the greatest miracle you have ever witnessed?

Are you presently struggling with a physical aliment that has tried to attach itself to your body?

Do you believe God is bigger than this condition (in question #12) and that He is able to remove it from your body?

Then, why not ask Him right now, no matter where you are, to set you free in the name of Jesus?

Chapter 21

On the Road to the Promised Land

Throughout this book I have written about the many roads I have traveled for the past sixty-seven years, and how I perceived things as a child, then a youth, and finally as an adult. Life definitely has been a journey for me.

There have been many exciting times and others I am thankful that God carried me through. However, the journey does not end here. I know there is so much more that lies ahead to which I look forward to with great expectation.

My journey started out on the road to Promise Land, which is an actual place. Promise Land is an area visited by many, and where others have lived, some for their entire lives. It is the place of their roots, their domain, a place many will never leave until the day they die.

Having been taught the Word of God, and knowing what I know today, I am persuaded that my journey is no longer one that at some point in time may lead me to Promise Land, but ultimately will lead me to the Promised Land!

"Let not your heart be troubled; you believe in God, believe also in Me. In My Father's house are many mansions; if it were not so, I would have

told you. I go to prepare a place for you. And if I go and prepare a place for you, I will come again and receive you to Myself; that where I am, there you may be also. And where I go you know, and the way you know." (John 14:1-4)

Here Jesus is saying that there is a road that leads to many mansions which have been built for us in the Promised Land. He has already gone there and left us with a GPS (Global Positioning System) - His Word.

"Jesus said to him, 'I am the way, the truth, and the life. No one comes to the Father except through Me.'" (John 14:6)

Although GPS systems have been out on the market for years, it was only recently that my wife purchased one for me. When the information of where I want to reach is programmed into this device, it is all set to give me detailed directions. It will advise me as to where I am presently located, how far I must travel to reach my destination, and what change of direction I will need to make to stay on course. It will also tell me approximately how long, in hours and minutes, it will take me to reach my destination. As long as I stay on course, I can be sure I'm headed in the right direction. However, if I make a wrong turn, it will announce, it will actually say that it is recalculating and redirecting me back onto course.

Having studied the Word for many years, I know there are promises God has made to His children. Through His Word, like a GPS, each person can know what the promises are that one needs to follow to reach his heavenly destination. Some of these I have not yet totally laid hold of, but I know **Mark 9:23** says: **"If you can believe, all things are possible to him who believes."** I believe and understand that age has nothing to do with believing, but I do agree that with age, experience, time with the Lord, and knowledge of His Word, one should grow in wisdom.

What wisdom have I gained through the years of walking with the Lord?

"Draw near to God and He will draw near to you..." (James 4:8a)

I know I am not as near to Him as He wants me to be. Understanding I am the one who needs to make the first move, I have taken some steps, and yet in my humanness, I have drawn back at times. This is not meant to be a negative confession, but it is the truth, and it is something I will have to continue working on for the rest of my life.

"Humble yourselves in the sight of the Lord, and He will lift you up." (James 4:10)

How hard it is to remain humble, but we know the Bible warns us that exalting ourselves will result in a disgraceful fall. Humbling ourselves leads to exaltation in this and the next world. It is His promise, if we humble ourselves and draw near to Him, He will lift us up.

Another principle and promise is:

"Give, and it shall be given to you: good measure, pressed down, shaken together, and running over will be put into your bosom. For with the same measure that you use, it will measured back to you." (Luke 6:38)

Here was a teaching that was very difficult for me to comprehend at first. As a child, then a youth, and finally a young adult, I had never been taught the principles stated in this verse of scripture, so I did not understand the principles of giving. However, I was taught at a very young age that in order to succeed in life, one had to work hard and to always give and do his best. Hard work was ingrained in my mind, but I had never totally understood what and to whom I was to give. At first this principle of giving my tithe to the Lord, my ten percent, stopped me in my tracks. That was way out of my way of doing things, and besides that, I was being encouraged to give offerings over and beyond my tithe.

"'Bring all the tithes into the storehouse, that there may be food in My house, and try Me now in this,' says the Lord of hosts ..." (Malachi 3:10a)

Having been rescued from financial bankruptcy, I decided to give it a try. God did say we should try Him. However, I did not start with ten percent, but I did as a pastor had shared with me about how he first began to tithe. He said, "If you do not feel comfortable with giving the ten percent, then start with three or four percent." He also stated that you should not remain at the rate you started, but should gradually increase it, and then not stop at the ten percent, but continue on, always increasing the tithe. The three percent was no problem, followed by the increase to four, then five and continuing up to ten.

Life throws many things at us, and financial obstacles will tempt us to give up, but the Word says that we are to give, even in the times of great need.

"But this I say: He who sows sparingly will also reap sparingly, and he who sows bountifully will also reap bountifully. So let each one give as he purposes in his heart, not grudgingly or of necessity; for God loves a cheerful giver." (II Corinthians 9:6-7)

This new road of giving up all to Him often calls for us to give, even when we ourselves have a need. It seems counter-productive, but giving out of our own need is God's way of clearing the avenues that He wants to use to bless us. Changing our attitude of giving is the key to unlocking the windows of heaven.

"'Will a man rob God? Yet you have robbed Me! But you say, "In what way have we robbed You?" In tithes and offerings. You are cursed with a curse, for you have robbed Me, even this whole nation. Bring all the tithes into the storehouse, that there may be food in My house, and try Me now in this,' says the Lord of hosts, 'If I will not open for you the windows of heaven and pour out for you such blessing that there will not be room enough to receive it. And I will rebuke the devourer for your sakes, so that he will not destroy the fruit of your ground, nor shall the vine fail to bear fruit for you in the field,' says the Lord of hosts." (Malachi 3:8-11)

One bit of wisdom I have gained over the many years of walking with the Lord is this:

"God is not a man, that He should lie, nor a son of man, that He should repent. Has He said, and will He not do? Or has He spoken, and will He not make it good?" (Numbers 23:19)

If we rob God, by not giving our whole tithe willfully and cheerfully, then we have nullified His promise to us as believers, and we should not look for heaven's open windows in our lives.

Here are some bits of wisdom that have had a positive influence on my life:

"No temptation has overtaken you except such as is common to man; but God is faithful, who will not allow you to be tempted beyond what you are able, but with the temptation will also make a way of escape, that you may able to bear it."
(I Corinthians 10:13)

It does not matter what road in life I am on, temptations will come my way, but, praise God, He will show me a way thorough these times of trials and tribulation and, **"No weapon formed against you (me) shall prosper." (Isaiah 54:17)**

"I know your works. See, I have set before you an open door, and no one can shut it; for you have a little strength, have kept My word, and have not denied My name." (Revelation 3:8)

Regardless of where I am, or who I am with, or what I do or say, He knows and sees all things. And it is He and He alone, who will set open doors before me.

"I know your works, that you are neither cold nor hot. I could wish you were cold or hot. So then, because you are lukewarm, and neither cold nor hot, I will vomit you out of My mouth."
(Revelation 3:15-16)

God is not going to settle for half-heartedness. He wants all or nothing, and He definitely wants no compromise of His Word.

**"If you love Me, keep My commandments. And I will pray the Father, and He will give you another Helper, that He may abide with you forever."
(John 14:15-16)**

"Another" here indicates one besides Jesus, one in addition to Him, one just like Jesus Christ, who in His absence will do what He would do if He were present with us.

"Let not your heart be troubled; you believe in God, believe also in Me. In My Father's house are many mansions; if it were not so, I would have told you. I go to prepare a place for you. And if I go and prepare a place for you, I will come again and receive you to Myself; that where I am, there you may be also. And where I go you know, and the way you know." (John 14:1-4)

Praise God, I will never be homeless! Oh, I may not have the finest of homes here on planet Earth, but someday I will be welcomed into my mansion in heaven.

What motivates me to do what I do? Jesus paid a price for me as He was nailed to the cross. He bought me out of slavery with His blood, set me free from all bondages, and I owe my life to Him.

Many years ago I cried out to God and said, "If you deliver me from this addiction, I'll serve you the rest of my life." Not only did He set me free; He cleansed me and filled me with His Spirit. He has commissioned me to go, and I will go as long as I have breath to breathe.

Responding to a Fire

I need to pause here as something has just happened outside my home which caught my attention. It was the sound of a fire truck with its sirens sounding as it was on the way to put out a fire. I don't know for certain where it was headed. I do know it was an emergency situation to which the firemen were responding.

Fires can result in the loss of property and sometimes the loss of life. Fires are for the most part destructive, but there are times they can be comforting and very useful. Living in South Texas we see first hand one of the benefits of a useful fire. The sugarcane stalk needs to have its outer growth removed when it is mature in order for it to become useful. This is done by a controlled fire being lit and burning off the leaves, leaving only the stalk, which becomes crystallized, making it ready for processing.

The Word of God gives many references to fire.

"A fire goes before Him, and burns up His enemies round about." (Psalm 97:3)

"When you pass through the waters, I will be with you; and through the rivers, they shall not overflow you. When you walk through the fire, you shall not be burned, nor shall the flame scorch you." (Isaiah 43:2)

"But who can endure the day of His coming? And who can stand when He appears? For He is a refiner's fire and like launderers' soap."
(Malachi 3:2)

"I indeed baptize you with water unto repentance, but He who is coming after me is mightier than I, whose sandals I am not worth to carry. He will baptize you with the Holy Spirit and fire."
(Matthew 3:11)

"For our God is a consuming fire."
(Hebrews 12:29)

Here in these verses of scripture, we first read that He is like a fire, which goes before us to burn up our enemies. Praise God, we don't have to walk in fear of our enemies. We can walk in His fullness and in His mercy and goodness.

Next the Word says that we will go through times of trial and tribulation. The heat will be turned up, but we will not be burned. There will not even be the smell of smoke on our bodies.

"No weapon formed against you shall prosper..."
(Isaiah 54:17a)

The Word also says that by His fire, we will be refined. All our impurities, all our imperfections will be burned up, and we will become like Him. We will be as precious as gold.

Finally, the Word says that He will baptize us with the Holy Spirit and fire. This is something we cannot do in our own strength. He has given us this right as His children. All we have to do is walk in obedience to His Word and ask, and this fire will become evident in our lives. How do we receive this fire? Simply by asking God in the name of Jesus to fill us with His Spirit.

Speaking of fires, it is almost daily that we read or hear about a fire burning out-of-control somewhere in the world. It appears that in many cases, no matter how hard the firefighters try, they are unable to bring it under control. They use every known method of trying to extinguish the fire. In some cases they will deliberately start another fire to cut off its supply of fuel. A fire cannot burn without a supply of fuel.

I have witnessed many people who were consumed by the fire of God. They were filled with the Holy Spirit and were on fire. They were unstoppable. They went and proclaimed the goodness of the Lord. It was not only with the words they spoke, but also with the lives they lived. But something happened. A deliberate fire was set by the enemy, and the fuel supply was cut off. They became too busy doing their own thing that they no longer had time for God and Jesus Christ. Gradually, little by little, the fire went out. They had lost focus of the course set before them. They had taken themselves out of the race.

Today, I don't see myself as a runner who has just completed a marathon. I see myself as a young runner standing at the gate of a cross-country race. What lies ahead for us? What road will we be traveling on as we depart on our next journey? One thing I know for certain, retirement is not an option. It is only an excuse that some choose, and it is not where I want to be found. Retirement, in my opinion, is like letting the fire go out in your life. Our future is in His hands, and time will reveal our next journey.

In conclusion, I want to challenge all of you who took the time to read this true life journey, to take a close look at the signs "on the road" in your life.

Hopefully, you will want to avoid going down the road that only leads to a dead end and the wrong destination. Hell is a destination. Perhaps you need to slow down and avoid skidding off the road due to weather-related conditions. Maybe it is the "dangerous curve ahead" sign which you need to focus on. Perhaps you have been cited for exceeding the speed limit. Why not slow down and take time to smell the roses along the way? Why not take a good look at what excessive baggage you are transporting?

Have you considered taking some time off, maybe doing some fishing and using the time as a time of casting and not just a time of reeling in?

"Cast all your care upon Him, for He cares for you." (I Peter 5:7)

The challenges you may be facing are not the end of the world for you, although they could be if you were to make an unwise decision. Let me encourage you to take a close look at where you are at this very moment. What do you see all around you? Is it love, joy, and peace, or do you find yourself standing in the midst of turmoil? Are you in the middle of a highly traveled intersection with cars passing by at a high rate of speed? Maybe you have reached that crossroad in your life, where you feel it's time for surrender, and you have no choice, but to raise the white flag, a sign of surrender, and to give up. But to whom are you going to surrender?

I know the feeling, because I once was there. I stood there not knowing which way to turn. I was lost, headed down the road to destruction. Hell had a welcome sign out for me. No way was I going to settle for Satan's lies.

Promise Land is a real place. People actually reside there. The Promised Land is a real place, too, just like hell is a real place. Although people presently live in Promise Land, that is not where they will spend eternity. It is only a temporary home. There is only one of two places everyone will spend eternity in, no matter of what the world may try to convince them. Eternity is either in heaven with Him, or forever separated from Him in hell.

Jesus has already gone before us and has prepared a place for us. Satan, the deceiver, has chosen to go in another direction, and this is the road of destruction and separation.

"The devil, who deceived them, was cast into the lake of fire and brimstone where the beast and the false prophet are. And they will be tormented day and night forever and ever." (Revelation 20:10)

Forever is a long time to be in constant torment and is not where I want to be found. Remember, it is only you who can make that decision of where you will spend eternity. All I can do is encourage you with the sincerity of my heart.

You can know for sure where you will spend eternity. How? By praying to God and asking Him to forgive you of all unrighteousness in your life.

Why not pray this prayer of repentance and know that you are "on the road to eternal life with Him?"

"Heavenly Father, I come to you in the name of Jesus. Lord, I admit I have sinned, and I want to turn from my sins. I believe You died on the cross for me. I believe You are the Son of God. I believe You rose from the dead and are seated at the right hand of God the Father. I repent for all those things I did and said against You, and I desire today to be born again. Amen."

If you just prayed that prayer and believe in your heart that you are set free from your sins, then you are a new creature in Christ. The old you is gone, and the new you has come. Now God will begin to reveal His plan for your life. You will be able to read His Word and understand it. Don't be afraid to tell others what you have done. We would love to hear from you.

The Word of God says, "that if you confess with your mouth the Lord Jesus and believe in your heart that God has raised Him from the dead, you will be saved." (Romans 10:9)

Questions Only You Can Answer

Chapter 21 "On the Road to the Promised Land"

Do you own a GPS?

How accurate do you find it to be?

Has it ever led you down a road that you knew you should not be on?

Do you struggle with "giving", and do you classify yourself as a robber?

Do you understand the principles of godly sowing, that what we sow will produce a harvest of like seed, whether it is positive or negative?

Do you know that no man or woman is exempt from times of testing?

Do you believe man has the ability to open some doors in life, but ultimately it is only God who can open the doors He has set before you?

Do you see yourself as a hot, lukewarm, or cold believer?

What assurance do you have of where you will spend eternity?

Do you, this day, see yourself "on the road to Promise Land" or "on the road to the Promised Land?"

Chapter 22

On the Road to a Time of Reflection

Nancy's Thoughts

This is great. I can relate my thoughts to you about this journey, the road to packing and unpacking suitcases, wondering where we will be headed next. As my husband stated, this book is about our journey with the Lord. I do have to say, I have had my own journey, and it has been a roller coaster ride at times.

I will reflect on just a few of the journeys the Lord has taken us on. I will call the rest of the book:

Still on the Journey

God moves in awesome ways when we least expect Him to do something. He is always faithful.

"A man's heart plans his way, but the Lord directs his steps." (Proverbs 16:9)

"The steps of a good man are ordered by the Lord, and He delights in his way." (Psalm 37:23)

I don't think anyone can totally comprehend everything the Lord is capable of doing. That is, unless you live by faith and live through all the times of challenges and victories. Believe me, there have been many times I have said, "Lord, you want me to do what?"

One of the most challenging roads on this journey has been the dying to self. What do I mean? Those things you see other people have, like family times and being connected to friends. Things like establishing a home, loving it and having to leave, sell it, giving it all up to follow God's leading. You have to be willing to say, "God, I want to serve you. Take all you want from me. It is yours anyway." It means giving up and dying to your wants, needs, and desires.

Submitting to the Lord has great rewards. Following Him is worth it all. If you are hesitating to do what God has asked you to do, my advice to you is simply this: have radical obedience.

I have to tell you this story. When we were walking in obedience, obeying God and collecting all that clothing and other goods, a man visited our home. He said:

> I have to tell you what happened to me. I took a walk in the woods one day. I was searching for direction in my life. As I sat there under a tree, I recall saying, "God, what do you want me to do for you?" I sat there for a few moments. I heard Him speak to my heart and say, "If I told you, would you do it?" I was so afraid He would ask me to do something I didn't want to do, that to this day I have not answered Him."

Does that sound like something you would say? There are times I don't know if I want to hear His voice, but I know it will be something good.

Radical obedience is obedience that takes you up the mountain of God. It is on this mountain that you will experience more of Him and see His mighty hand at work.

"On the Road to an Indian Village in Mexico"

First, let me set the stage. There were two vans headed for an unknown territory in Mexico. There were times when we all had to get out of the vans and push our vehicle through water and gullies. We questioned the Lord, "What are we in for this time?" Would you believe along the way to our destination, the vans got separated. My husband was driving the first one. I was riding in the second one, and we got separated. We did not panic, but prayed that somehow, as we saw the fork in the road ahead, we would know which way to go.

When we arrived at the crossroad, there stood a person with an outstretched arm pointing a finger in the direction we were to go. We didn't stop or ask any questions. We just went in the direction we had received. This person came out of nowhere. God had sent an angel to show us the way, and when we followed that leading, we were united with the rest of the team.

This was a very remote village in Mexico. It was here that we visited in one woman's house to pray with her. It was the hardest prayer I ever had to pray. She wanted us to pray for God to give her a new home. The one she lived in was made out of small thin sticks. You could see the outside light through the walls. The floors were dirt, and there was a hammock for a bed. How do you do that? How do you pray for God to give her a new house in this remote area? Was it possible? That would take faith that moves mountains. I didn't know if God would answer our prayer. All I knew is that all things are possible when you believe.

After leaving that village we started out on another journey. We were on the road to our next God-encounter. My husband had passed many gas stations before getting to this remote area. We were in the wilderness, and there was no gas in the van. We saw a roadside stand, which only had a few snacks and some sodas, but no gasoline. We stood around for just a short while, and wouldn't you know it, God showed up again. We heard a car coming, a battered old car, and it pulled in alongside of us. The man said something in Spanish, which we did not understand, and then he went to the rear of the car, opened the trunk, and in there was a five gallon can full of gas! This man and the gas came out of nowhere. We had a team of people who stood there in total awe! Another angel in disguise. You may wonder how far the five gallons of gas took us. We made it into the parking lot of the next gas station, and there we ran out of gas. The team had to push the van for the final few feet to the pump, but we made it.

"On the Road to God's Opening Doors"

God will put you before kings and officials. God showed us a need, the need being a home for the elderly, a huge place being built which would house many people. The project was being headed up by the president's wife of the city we lived in, which was Matehuala, Mexico.

In that country, high ranking officials are referred to as presidents. This president's wife's number one mission was to get this home built in the three years her husband was in office. We visited with them many times, taking them food, two whirlpool tubs to be used for therapy, and medical supplies. Bedding was also needed for this home. (The beds were flat slabs made out of concrete.)

God supernaturally supplied all our needs once again. A church in Pennsylvania shipped sheets and blankets to us, and we were able to be a blessing to these people. When they had the grand opening of the home, we were honored guests of the president and his wife. This was another God-opportunity. Mission accomplished! Do you recognize God-opportunities, and do you take advantage of them with thanksgiving?

Who would think we would be able to communicate without speaking the language and build two large churches in Mexico? When the churches were built, all digging had to be done by hand. All concrete had to be mixed by hand, and we had to use five gallon buckets on ropes to get the concrete to the second floor. Lots of blood, sweat, and tears were shed. Many teams from the United States were organized with people having to use their vacation times and others taking time off without pay from their jobs to come and help with the projects.

"And my God shall supply all your need according to His riches in glory by Christ Jesus."
(Philippians 4:19)

At one point in time we needed an electrician to do a lot of wiring. We were introduced to a man in the United States who said he was an electrician from West Virginia. It was not long before he and his wife joined with us to do the work. In our conversation, he mentioned that he ministered to the youth at the church they attended. Immediately, we arranged for him to minister to the youth, and today he is a youth pastor.

What is God speaking to your heart that you have been procrastinating about? God puts ideas and plans in our hearts, and He expects us to act on them. Maybe you are waiting for the right moment. Maybe you are waiting for someone to come your way and invite you to step out in faith to begin to fulfill your God-given purpose. I have to tell you that many times we pray like this: "God, open doors for me." He hears your prayer, but I have to tell you, He is waiting on you to step out with a plan to accomplish what He has placed in your heart, and when you do, the doors will open. If you think God can't or won't use you, it is wrong thinking. Just be available and willing.

Our entire life has been about miracles. God miracles! Sometimes we forget about what God has done in our lives. I forgot how He used us to minister to thousands of children in mountain villages, towns, and orphanages in all the countries we ministered. As they heard about Jesus, they prayed and accepted Him as their Savior. Recently, I came across a box of photos, and the memories were overwhelming as I saw pictures of all the children's faces, many with uplifted hands. I looked at pictures of men, women, and teens who were ministered to and many who received their healing.

God used us to train teenagers how to minister to children by using object lessons, stories, games, and costume characters. The teens were excited as we gave them costumes like Yogi, Boo-Boo, Clowns, Mini and Mickey, and many others to wear. The teens who assisted us were very creative in their ideas. They did face-painting that looked professional, and the fun they had doing it was very exciting to everybody. God supernaturally supplied all our needs for these outreaches. Many days we would drive three hours one way to reach the ranch where we would minister. I am writing this to encourage you to believe God to be a God of supernatural supply and a God of miracles.

God took us to the Philippines where we rode in a vehicle called a Jeepney. It resembles what we know as a Jeep in our country. The biggest difference is that these vehicles only have metal seats to sit on. This was our means of transportation as we had to travel many hours to get to the place where we were ministering. In one of these villages, a woman put something in my hand. It was a piece of paper and on it was written the names of people she wanted me to pray for. There was also some money in this note. I believe it may have been all she had at that time.

There were many heartbreaking happenings on this trip. As we were about to leave one village, a woman handed us her baby and asked us to take care of her child. Of course, we had to say no. If this was not hard enough, one of the boys from the orphanage ran after our vehicle, weeping, and stretching out his hand to us. It was the first time in our lives we hesitated before boarding a plane for our flight home. We wept for four days.

On this road of reflection of what God has done, we remember many accepting Jesus as their Savior through the Christmas and Easter dramas we wrote and directed. God has taken us from five star hotels to storage areas, where we slept. He has taken us from ministering to hundreds of people to a place where we taught leadership to pastors and their wives in a tin storage building. He has allowed us to see needs and meet needs. Not everything God does will be big and grand. Taking food to a family every week for a year or buying bananas for the children may be all He requires of us. God used us to build houses and outside bathrooms. For a while I thought God was putting us in the housing business.

This has been a journey of a lifetime, which began by being obedient to His voice. Sometimes I said, "God, let me off this ride." At times it all goes so fast. Maybe I shouldn't have asked God, "What's next?"

Remember, I am taking you on a journey of reflection. Can you believe God told us to hold a conference for pastors in a location which once housed a Bible school? This one had been closed for years. Needless to say there were many repairs needed, and everything had to be cleaned to prepare the facility. Our team of cooks prepared food for the pastors and their families for four days. There was fellowship, unity, and leadership teaching to strengthen and encourage the pastors and their families.

The Lord sent us a doctor who had a desire to help ill people in remote villages of Mexico. Hundreds of dollars of medicines were taken, and hundreds of people received help. What an awesome sight to see as we pulled into a village, and people were gathered to see the doctor. This was a perfect example of a "country doctor." Those traveling with us helped the doctor by taking blood pressures and temperatures and handing out the medicines. The doctor would spend hours with the patients, and the people would wait for hours to see the doctor. We would visit different villages and return to many of them, to follow-up on the conditions of the people. Our oldest patient was 102 years old. Many medical missions were done over several years, and many blessings were given to the people. Besides medicines, we had treats for the people, and the skin care products were a big hit.

We also traveled many miles, visiting locations where we taught the leadership principles, "Training Leaders in the Nations to Make a Difference."

God has taken us from being on the pastoral staff of a church of over 15 hundred people to the mission field, to an opportunity to work for a huge ministry in St. Louis, Missouri.

What a ride! Remember, when you yield yourself to God, He will use you in ways you never thought He would or could.

I know all of you reading this book have stories to tell. If you are asking God to show you your purpose, if you are asking Him to use you, get ready, get going, and don't look back.

We pray you are encouraged and in awe of our awesome God. He will do the same for you as He has done for us. The journeys we are on, and the ones you are on, are not over. God has more surprises in store. Don't stop praying and seeking Him. If you are in the wilderness wondering if God hears your prayers, keep on pressing in, until you hear that still small voice. He will direct you to the path of victory.

Remember, God is looking for total obedience, not partial obedience. What God has and is presently doing in our lives, He will do for you. Trust Him, and He will direct you as you travel "on the road to your journey."

Have you ever wondered what God is doing? Have you been traveling on a road, and you forgot where you were going? You may forget or wonder why God is taking you in a different direction or wonder where you will end up. This is true, especially if you take a wrong turn, but God really does know the way.

The journey you are on is sometimes difficult to under-stand. There may be detours. When you see the signs, you need to follow the directions, and you will ultimately arrive at your God-directed destination.

Don't give up! Hang on, because you may be in for the ride of your life. You are not in it alone. It may feel like you are alone, but God promises you victory and arrival at the destination He has for you. One thing you want to remember is, when you trust God for directions, don't try to tell Him which way to go. Just yield!

To contact the author:

Rev. Roger R. Rinker
248 Diana Drive
Alamo, Texas
78516-2572

e-mail rink6@juno.com

When contacting us please include your testimony or the help you have received from reading this book. Your prayer concerns are always welcomed.

CPSIA information can be obtained at www.ICGtesting.com
Printed in the USA
BVOW07s1953220115

384544BV00001B/3/P